Soft Skills

by Cindi Reiman

for **dummies**®

A Wiley Brand

Soft Skills For Dummies®

Published by: **John Wiley & Sons, Inc.**, 111 River Street, Hoboken, NJ 07030-5774, www.wiley.com

For general information on our other products and services, please contact our Customer Care Department within the U.S. at 877-762-2974, outside the U.S. at 317-572-3993, or fax 317-572-4002. For technical support, please visit https://hub.wiley.com/community/support/dummies.

Wiley publishes in a variety of print and electronic formats and by print-on-demand. Some material included with standard print versions of this book may not be included in e-books or in print-on-demand. If this book refers to media such as a CD or DVD that is not included in the version you purchased, you may download this material at http://booksupport.wiley.com. For more information about Wiley products, visit www.wiley.com.

Library of Congress Control Number: 2022949715

ISBN: 978-1-119-90655-1 (pbk); ISBN 978-1-119-90657-5 (ebk); ISBN 978-1-119-90656-8 (ebk)

SKY10038394_111522

Contents at a Glance

Table of Contents

Introduction

The world and workforce have changed. Now more than ever, today's employers are after more than technical ability or hard skills; they're looking for real team players who have strong interpersonal communication skills and who demonstrate resourcefulness and leadership in the workplace.

A college degree no longer guarantees you a successful career. *Transitional skills,* also known as *soft skills,* are also now required — indeed, are often more highly desired — across all industries. In fact, companies such as Google, EY (Ernst & Young), and IBM are now actively recruiting candidates without traditional academic qualifications, preferring to hire for attitude and train for aptitude. Becoming the best and most attractive employee you can be starts with becoming the best and most attractive person you can be. *Soft Skills For Dummies* is specifically designed to help you prepare to enter or reenter the workforce by providing a comprehensive guide to the essential employability traits and soft skills needed for success in the in 21st century workplace. This book's goal is to help you cultivate the ten essential personal attributes attractive to future employers: attitude, character, communication, cultural awareness, appearance and etiquette, time management, teamwork, work ethic, critical thinking, and leadership.

About This Book

Working and playing nice with others and being a nice person — using soft skills — doesn't come naturally to everyone, but you can acquire these skills. The problem is knowing where to do that. Many schools don't teach them, and employers often don't have time to train their employees in them. I wasn't taught them on my first job but I was expected to have them when I was hired; thanks to my parents, who both came from the school of *play nice and be nice and life will be nice back to you,* I did. But unfortunately, most of the young people I encountered when I started my business didn't.

I witnessed the skills gap firsthand and set out to create a training program designed to help promising young professionals become better and happier employees tomorrow — and better and happier people today — through cultivating ten basic personality skills. Those ten simple people skills are the cornerstone of my company's training program, which has successfully served thousands of college interns around the world, and now create the foundation of this book.

The ten soft skills I cover here show that. fostering a strong soft skills set helps put you on the road to career success. Soft skills may not get you the job of your dreams, because you also need hard skills. However, soft skills can help get you in the door, and they definitely can help you keep that job and advance in the workplace.

Foolish Assumptions

Although making assumptions can lead to misunderstandings, I did make a few in writing this book. For the sake of clarity, though, I'm stating them right here. I've assumed that you

>> Want to become more attractive to future employers

>> Are looking to improve your workplace and life skills

>> Aspire to become a better and happier employee and person

>> Are willing to reflect on what you read and put it into practice

Icons Used in This Book

TIP

The Tip icon marks tips (duh!) and shortcuts that you can use to make putting your soft skills to use easier.

REMEMBER

Remember icons mark the information that's especially important to know. I often identify the most important information in each chapter with these icons, so pay special attention to this information.

WARNING

The Warning icon tells you to watch out! It marks important information that may save you headaches.

Beyond the Book

In addition to the abundance of information and guidance about soft skills that I provide in this book, you get access to more help and information online at https://dummies.com. The Cheat Sheet is a convenient resource to remind yourself what the ten essential soft skills are and offers some basic ways you can work to make using them a habit.

Just go to https://dummies.com and search for **Soft Skills For Dummies** to find a handy online cheat sheet as well as books and articles on other subjects that you may find useful.

Where to Go from Here

Well, Chapter 1 is a great place to start! There I give you an overview of soft skills and their importance to career and life success, along with a brief introduction to each of the ten individual soft skills I detail in later chapters.

I've designed Chapters 2 through 11 to help you discover, cultivate, and demonstrate the ten soft skills essential to professional and personal achievement. Some of the skills are more personal, and some are more practical, so you can skip around these chapters based on whether you want to improve your life skills or your employability skills.

For example, if you need an attitude check and want to read up on daily affirmations, flip to Chapter 2. If improving your time management skills is something you know can help you in your current job, start with Chapter 7.

You see where I'm going here: Make this book work for you! It doesn't matter where you start. It only matters that you do! After all, you've got workplaces to go to and future employers to meet.

1

Laying Down a Solid Foundation with Soft Skills

IN THIS PART . . .

Figure out what soft skills are.

Develop the right attitude as the basis for your other soft skills.

Recognize that your character matters and put in the work to build a good one.

Chapter 1

Seeing What Soft Skills Are All About

Today's employers are seeking more from their employees than technical knowledge and expertise. They also are looking for people who are willing to work as team players, who possess strong communication and problem-solving skills, and who demonstrate good character, good work ethic, strong leadership, and a positive attitude in the workplace. In short, they're looking for employees with soft skills.

In this chapter, I define soft skills, introduce you to our ten most important soft skills, and discuss why cultivating a strong soft skills set is essential to career and life success

The term soft skills *itself is just jargon. From the standpoint of behavioral science, it really refers to a series of mindsets and behaviors.*

—ERIC FRAZER, *AUTHOR OF* THE PSYCHOLOGY OF TOP TALENT

Where Do People Learn Soft Skills?

Most people in the United States don't learn soft skills in school . . . at least not after elementary school. In preschool and early elementary school, students experience role modeling and instruction on soft skills daily. Children learn how to interact with classmates, approach assignments, manage time, and organize their desks and backpacks. They learn about the importance of good character and having a positive attitude. By the time students get to middle school, focus shifts to learning in content area coursework and preparing for high school, where college transcripts and grade point averages are the priority.

Despite decades of research demonstrating the critical role soft skills play in executing hard skills, for the most part high school and college students don't get resources that can help them identify, develop, and master these important personal skills. Students may still pick up soft skills through participation in athletics and extracurricular activities, but they don't receive deliberate instruction for developing the skills that make all other skills work their best.

Newly hired employees enter the workplace with the hard skills they need, but they haven't been given the opportunity to cultivate the essential soft skills that enable their hard skills to work more effectively and successfully.

Obviously, a wide gap exists between what education currently teaches and what industry now requires where soft skills are concerned, and that's where this book comes in! I wrote *Soft Skills For Dummies* to bridge that gap and give first-time job seekers and those returning to the workforce the soft skills education today's employers are so desperately seeking.

What Are Soft Skills?

Think of the difference between hard and soft skills this way: *Hard skills* are what you do. *Soft skills* are how you do what you do. They're the personal character traits, qualities, and habits that make you uniquely you. Your work ethic, your attitude, and the way you interact with other people are a few examples of soft skills. They're the personal and interpersonal skills you bring with you to work and apply to your life every day.

Some soft skills are somewhat subjective by nature, such as your attitude, your character, and your appearance and etiquette. And some soft skills are more objective or practical, such as time management, work ethic, cultural awareness and critical thinking. When the subjective and the objective/practical come together, they work in harmony to help you become not only a more well-rounded employee but also a more well-rounded person.

Cultivating a complete, strong soft skills set can make a significant positive impact on both your immediate and long-term career and life success. In fact, after your soft skills set becomes as good as (or better than) your hard skills set, you're all set to achieve great things. You don't just survive in the workplace and in the world; you thrive!

If you ask people which of the soft skills is most important, you may find that different people rank different skills as number one. However, the general consensus is that the following ten are the essential skills you should work on developing.

Attitude

Your attitude, not your aptitude, determines your success in the workplace and in life. A positive attitude is necessary no matter what kind of job you have. Being optimistic and determined are the essence of what you need for career and life achievement, which is why more and more companies today look for attitude among job candidates. The company can later train for aptitude. You can read more about cultivating this soft skill in Chapter 2.

Character

Good character doesn't just happen. You develop your character every day by the choices you make in all you do. Flip to Chapter 3 for details on fostering this skill.

Diversity and cultural awareness

Having *cultural awareness* means you embrace diversity in the workplace and accept and appreciate differences among the people you work with. Cultivating cultural awareness allows you to effectively and successfully socialize and work with people from a wide range of cultural backgrounds. Chapter 5 has more info on cultural awareness.

Communication

Poor communication can lead to misunderstandings, hurt feelings, and costly errors both in the workplace and in your personal life. To effectively communicate with others, you need them to clearly understand both your words and the actions that accompany them. You can read more about this soft skill in Chapter 4.

Appearance and etiquette

Four seconds: That's all you take to make a first — and lasting — impression on those you meet. Your appearance and your etiquette are often major factors in that initial impression, so think about what kind of first impression you want to make. I discuss these topics more in Chapter 6.

Time management

Being on time — whether you're arriving for an appointment or turning in a deadline-driven project — is important both professionally and personally. If you know someone who always arrives late, you may have first-hand experience with the frustration poor time management can cause. Check out Chapter 7 for details on managing your time rather than letting it manage you.

Teamwork

You may have heard the saying "There's no *I* in team." The ability to work and play well with others is essential because very few people work and live without needing to cooperate with others to reach a goal. After all, the ultimate goal of any company is to achieve overall effectiveness, but this strategy succeeds only when everyone on the team works together toward the same target. I cover this skill in Chapter 8.

Work ethic

People aren't born with a good work ethic. Each person has to make a choice to work hard regardless of whether they love what they're doing or when it feels like a chore. When you demonstrate a good work ethic, those around you are more likely to notice and reward your effort. You can read more about strengthening this soft skill in Chapter 10.

Critical thinking and problem solving

The ability to think for yourself and take ownership of your choices and decisions leads to a better understanding of the world and your place in it. Having your own point of view helps you make decisions to achieve successful outcomes, solve problems that arise, and communicate more effectively with others. Head to Chapter 9 for a deeper dive into these skills.

Leadership

You demonstrate leadership through your everyday actions and interactions with others. A leader is effective because of who they are on the inside and how their personal qualities reflect on the outside. You don't necessarily need a special set of talents to take a leadership role, but you do need to have a willingness to step forward to take responsibility for directing and encouraging other people. We cover this soft skill in Chapter 11.

What's the Big Deal about Soft Skills?

Soft skills go by many different names — people skills, core skills, human skills, 21st-century skills, transitional skills, employability traits, and interpersonal skills. You'll most likely encounter some or all of these terms on job applications and in job interviews. The terms may change from company to company, but the meaning behind them is the same, and it's very simple: Soft skills make the hard skills work.

REMEMBER

Soft skills make the hard skills work. This phrase bears repeating, and I use it often throughout this book. I hope you take it to heart so you can demonstrate it confidently and successfully in the workplace and in life.

Here's one way to look at it: Imagine buying some property at the top of a hill, but after you've made the purchase, you realize the path to get there is treacherous and overgrown. To get there, you have to clear the path, which will ultimately make traveling up and down the hill easier and more enjoyable. It will also make your property more appealing to other people. You have the hard skills you need to clear the path to the top, but do you have the personal perseverance to do the hard work? Do you have the positive attitude to enjoy the task? Do you have the character to keep your eye on the prize until you reach the very top?

Well, that's where soft skills come in.

REMEMBER

Soft skills can help you polish that ladder and really make it shine. Soft skills can make that ladder — and the goal at the top — look so pretty, so exciting, and so much fun that you can't wait to start your climb. Soft skills can also make your hard skills shinier and more attractive to prospective employers and to other people.

That's right. Soft skills improve your performance and opportunity for success not only in the workplace but also in life.

And in case you think the focus on soft skills is a hot trend in the business community that will soon burn itself out, I'm here to tell you that they've been important to workplace success for many, many years, as the following studies show:

>> More than 100 years ago, the Carnegie Foundation for the Advancement of Teaching released a study on engineering education authored by Charles Riborg Mann. In this study, 1,500 engineers replied to a questionnaire about what they believed to be the most important factors in determining probable success or failure as an engineer. Overwhelmingly, personal qualities (that is, soft skills) were considered seven times more important than knowledge of engineering science.

>> In the spring of 2006, the Conference Board, Corporate Voices for Working Families, the Partnership for 21st Century Skills, and the Society for Human Resource Management conducted an in-depth study on the corporate perspective of the new entrants' readiness for the U.S. workforce. The survey results indicated that far too many young people were inadequately prepared to be successful in the workplace. The report found that well over half of new high school–level workforce entrants were insufficiently prepared in the following workplace skills: oral and written communication, professionalism, work ethics, and critical thinking/problem solving.

>> In a 2021 review of more than 80 million job postings across 22 industry sectors, the educational nonprofit organization America Succeeds discovered that almost two-thirds of job listings included soft skills among their qualifications, and seven of the ten most in-demand skills were soft. The same report found that certain professions, including management and business operations, actually prioritize soft skills.

GETTING A LITTLE OXYGEN

Once upon a time, the powers that be at Google — yep, that gigantic, multibillion-dollar company that much of the world relies on to answer questions in a matter of seconds — were only interested in employee candidates who had graduated from top computer science programs. The company's focus was all about the technology. Brains and book smarts, also known as hard skills.

At least that's what the managers at Google thought was most important when they decided which candidates to hire.

Then Google decided to test this hiring hypothesis by crunching every bit and byte of hiring, firing, and promotion data accumulated since the company's incorporation in 1983. The effort was called Project Oxygen, and the results of this multiyear study shocked company executives. The eight top characteristics of success at Google were all found to be soft skills:

- Being a good coach
- Empowering the team and avoiding micromanagement
- Expressing interest in others
- Being productive and results-oriented
- Being a good communicator
- Helping employees with career development
- Having clear vision and strategy for the team
- Having the hard skills needed to help advise the team

Technical expertise came in at number eight.

You read that right. Google determined the most successful employees weren't simply good at computer science; each and every one of them, every single day on the job, displayed seven personality characteristics: leadership, teamwork, good communication, problem-solving, good work ethic, adaptability, and interpersonal skills. In other words: soft skills.

This story is totally true. Go ahead. Google it.

How Do You Apply Soft Skills to Work and Life?

It's a fact: Having a college degree no longer guarantees a successful career. Transitional (soft) skills are now requirements for employee candidates, and sometimes they're even more important than that piece of paper from an educational institution. Companies such as Google, EY (formerly Ernst & Young), and IBM now frequently recruit candidates without academic qualifications, and other companies such as Apple and Starbucks also have begun to realize that they need to diversify this aspect of their workforces.

When you look at people who don't go to school and make their way in the world, those are exceptional human beings. And we should do everything we can to find those people.

—LASZLO BOCK, FORMER SENIOR VICE PRESIDENT OF
PEOPLE OPERATIONS AT GOOGLE

TIP

Although having a college degree can provide satisfaction just for being a tremendous achievement, simply having that degree doesn't cut it for career and life success and satisfaction. The nonacademic things you've learned both in traditional school and in the school of life and how you choose to demonstrate that knowledge are what really matter.

Building a strong set of soft skills can be harder than acquiring a hard skill set because soft skills have very little to do with technical knowledge or expertise, which you can often get through memorization and testing. Acquiring soft skills requires constant conscious effort, ongoing practice, and a commitment to personal and professional self-development.

To hone your soft skills, you have to work on them every single day to see clear results. You have to recognize the importance of soft skills and take your development of them personally because no one is going to do it for you.

But it's worth it. I promise. And there's no time like the present!

A person often becomes what he believes himself to be. If I keep on saying to myself that I cannot do a certain thing, it is possible that I may end by really becoming incapable of doing it. On the contrary, if I have the belief that I can do it, I shall surely acquire the capacity to do it, even if I may not have it at the beginning.

—MAHATMA GANDHI

DON'T HOLD BACK

A company's CEO was very strict and often disciplined the workers for their mistakes or perceived lack of progress. One day, as the employees came into work, they saw a sign on the door that read, "Yesterday, the person who has been holding you back from succeeding in this company passed away. Please gather for a funeral service in the assembly room."

Although the employees were saddened for the family of their CEO, they were also intrigued at the prospect of now being able to move up within the company and become more successful.

When they entered the assembly room, many employees were surprised to see the CEO there. They wondered, "If it wasn't the CEO who has been holding us back from being successful, who was it? Who has died?"

One by one, the employees approached the coffin and looked inside. They didn't understand what they saw.

In the coffin was a mirror. So when each employee looked in to find out who'd been holding them back from being successful, each person saw their own reflection. Next to the mirror was a sign that read, "The only person who's able to limit your growth is you."

You're the only person who can influence your success. Your life changes when you break through your limiting beliefs and realize that you're in control of your life. The most influential relationship you can have is the relationship you have with yourself.

You can't blame anyone else if you're not living up to your potential. You can't let other people get you down about mistakes you make or their negative perception of your efforts. You have to take personal responsibility for your work — both the good and the bad — and be proactive about making any necessary adjustments.

Chapter 2

Going Far with a Great Attitude

Most people are about as happy as they make up their minds to be.

The process of cultivating a strong set of *soft skills* — the personal skills that are essential to workplace and life success — can be as hard or as easy as you make it. Yep, it all starts with you. It starts inside you with the attitude you choose each day.

You have two choices: positive or negative. And choosing what attitude you adopt is the most important choice you make each day. Sometimes you have to make that choice several times in a day, which is something I talk about later in this chapter. Consequently, *attitude is everything.* Get your attitude right from the get-go, and you're good to go.

In this chapter, I explain how to recognize and display successful personal and professional work attitudes; how to develop realistic expectations for yourself in the workplace; and how to cultivate and demonstrate a positive attitude that improves your chances of succeeding in everything you do both in the workplace and in life.

Accentuating the Positive

Sure, it's easy to say, "Be positive." But when you're out in the real world, dealing with the inevitable ups and downs of everyday life, it's not always easy to do. So I'm not going to simply tell you to be positive, and we're not going to promise you that the sun will come out tomorrow. Instead, I want to inspire you to choose to find a way to be positive no matter what comes your way.

Attitude defines your outlook and your approach to life. Your attitude influences everything you say and do, and everything you say and do determines your success. It's that old "is the glass half full or half empty?" question, which only you can answer for yourself. If your attitude is negative, pessimistic, or self-defeating, you may allow workplace and life opportunities that come your way to pass you by. If your attitude is positive, hopeful, excited, and energetic, you're going to swing open life's door every time opportunity knocks! And you're going to go places. I promise.

REMEMBER

Your attitude also determines how you relate to and interact with others at work, at home, and out in the world. Despite what you may have heard, in this case, opposites absolutely *do not* attract. Positive people attract positive people, and they want to work with positive people. Negative people don't attract anyone. And to be honest, no one wants to work or play with them, either. Fortunately, you can always turn negatives into positives. All it takes is desire and a little bit of work.

Recognizing the Importance of a Positive Attitude

Whether your attitude is positive or negative determines how you react to every situation life throws at you. Regardless of whether a situation is good or bad, if you choose to approach it with a positive attitude, 99 percent of the time you're going to respond in positive and productive ways.

I'm not saying it's easy. Life hands you lots of negatives along with the positives. Grumpy co-workers, lousy weather, lousier traffic, stress, disappointments, work and life failures — they can all add up and bring you down. However, positive attitudes are powerful. A person with a positive attitude recognizes the co-worker's grumpy exterior, realizes that they just aren't having a good day, and chooses to overlook it. Or, better yet, to send them a smile. A person with a positive attitude can figure out a way to use the traffic downtime to their advantage and see work and life failures as learning opportunities. They can tell themselves they did their best, smile in their heart, and move onward and upward.

Having a positive attitude takes work and a lot of practice, but it's a critical soft skill to develop. Having a good attitude can not only make work easier but it's also the foundation for some of the other soft skills that I talk about later in this book, such as being a team player. When you work to look for the good in any situation and find the positive, the results of your effort are worth it.

The following sections explain the benefits of staying positive.

Singing the praises of a positive attitude

When you turn a frowny attitude upside down, you see immediate results. Your life and your career start going places. You and your positive attitude start to get noticed (in a good way) by people who matter. Because for achieving workplace and life success, nothing beats being a positive person.

Here's what can happen when you exhibit a positive attitude at work:

>> You contribute to increased morale and teamwork.

>> Your productivity increases.

>> You're accepting of change and new policies.

>> You contribute to a solution-oriented work environment.

>> You find greater exposure to career opportunities and upward mobility.

>> You demonstrate professionalism.

>> You communicate a positive image to potential customers, clients, staff, and guests.

Here's what happens when you employ your positive attitude at play:

>> You appreciate the little things.

>> You try new things.

>> You distance yourself from negative people.

>> You find your passions.

>> You find things to believe in.

- » You have a ton of energy.
- » You want to make others happy.
- » You smile and laugh. A lot!
- » You have a curious mind.
- » You have better health.

REMEMBER

At the end of the day, whether you're at work or play, positivity is an attitude of *success*. Negativity is an attitude of *failure*.

Remembering your attitude determines your altitude

Whether you believe you can do a thing or not, you are right.

—HENRY FORD, AUTOMOTIVE PIONEER

Regardless of whether you're searching for a career path, you're just starting out on your chosen path, or you've gotten stalled or derailed along the way and are starting your job journey all over again, remember that your attitude determines your altitude at work and in life. Adjusting your attitude is essential to adjusting your altitude. How high and how far you can go in the workplace is something you largely determine, and it requires that you go the extra mile. That may mean arriving to work early or staying late every once in a while. It may mean taking an extra shift when things are busy. It may mean enrolling at your local community college to earn a certificate or degree to climb the workplace ladder, which means you may have to find a way to go to school and work at the same time.

A positive attitude goes a long way to helping you figure out how to climb the workplace ladder to career and life success. Night school, online courses, financial assistance — the opportunities to soar personally and professionally are out there if you're willing to put effort into pursuing them and think positively about your ability to succeed at them.

When you learn how to adjust your attitude — how to think about all the ways you *can* rather than all the ways you *can't* — your altitude will adjust accordingly, and you'll fly.

Taking an Attitude Check

People with an A+ attitude always outshine those who possess the hard skills ("the know-how") required to get work and life done but never show enthusiasm or passion while they're getting it done ("the go-how").

Are you ready to find out where you land on the attitude scale today? Are you brimming with go-how, or do you have room for a little attitude adjustment? For the following statements, a score of 1 means "not at all," and a score of 5 means "this is totally me." Record your score for each item to see where you fall on the attitude scale.

My life is exciting and fun.				
1	2	3	4	5

I love my job.				
1	2	3	4	5

My laughter index is high.				
1	2	3	4	5

I have an attitude of gratitude for all the good in my life.				
1	2	3	4	5

People find my passion and positive attitude infectious.				
1	2	3	4	5

I have passionate hobbies or special interests.				
1	2	3	4	5

My job is aligned to my strengths and allows me to do what I do best every day.				
1	2	3	4	5

The workday often flies by because I'm so excited about what I'm doing.				
1	2	3	4	5

I look forward to my future.				
1	2	3	4	5

Scoring:

40 to 50 points: Your positive attitude level is soaring.

26 to 39 points: Remember, you have a choice each day on how you live it.

10 to 25 points: Your attitude can use a major adjustment. Take a look at the earlier sections in this chapter. Even just a skim. Everything you need to start your climb is right here.

REMEMBER

I can tell you all day long that attitude is everything, but to achieve real career and life success, you need to check in with your attitude every so often to determine where you are on the positivity scale so you can decide whether you need make an adjustment or just keep on rocking it!

Sporting a Positive Attitude: The Smart Choice

No matter what's going on in their life, everyone has the opportunity to choose how they're going to react. Every single moment of your life, you have a choice to be caring or uncaring, calm or angry, open or judgmental, attentive or dismissive, respectful or full of disdain. You can choose to focus on what's right and to make good choices from the options you have in any given situation.

REMEMBER

In other words, your attitude isn't something you just set and forget. It doesn't operate on automatic pilot. Your attitude is influenced by the choices you make all day every day. You have to check it — and sometimes adjust it — throughout the day in everything you do and with everyone you meet.

Looking on the bright side

Every single day, every single person gets a blank slate, a brand-new start. And that includes you! Each morning you get to decide what kind of attitude you bring to your job and your life. You can choose a moody attitude and have a depressing and dark day. You can choose a grouchy attitude and use it to irritate your co-workers and customers. Or you can choose a sunny, playful, cheerful attitude and make it a great day for yourself and others!

The world is like a mirror; frown at it, and it frowns at you. Smile, and it smiles, too.

The following story demonstrates how choosing different attitudes influences the way you think and act.

The Three Bricklayers

It's a hot summer day, the kind of day when the sun seems to be intensified by a magnifying glass. Walking along the steamy street, you come across a construction site where almost everyone has chosen to work in the shade. Only three bricklayers work in the sun.

Makes sense to you, right? Still, you wonder about the bricklayers out in the hot sun. What's their story? So you step up and ask them, "What are you doing working out in this hot sun? Wouldn't you rather be in the shade taking it easy with everyone else?"

The first bricklayer answers gruffly, "Can't you see? I'm laying bricks."

The second bricklayer glances your way and replies, "It's my job. I'm putting up a wall."

The third bricklayer stands and wipes a bead of sweat from their brow, looks you right in the eye, smiles, and says with pride, "I'm creating a cathedral. It will stand forever and inspire people to do great deeds."

REMEMBER

The moral of this story? You always have choice about the perspective you have on your work. Even if you don't have a choice about the work itself or your co-workers, you can choose how you feel about it and how you do it. So how do you make the best of a not-so-hot situation? I offer some tips in the following sections.

Adjusting your attitude when your job brings you down

A wise person once wrote that the key to having a good attitude is the willingness to change your thinking. Here are few ways to maintain a positive attitude when you aren't passionate about the work:

» **Make a list of the things you *do* like about your work.** You may not like certain aspects of your job, but focusing instead on the things you *do* like makes the work less of a chore. And if you can't find anything you like about the work you do, ask a few of your co-workers what they like about the job. Sometimes, a different perspective can help you find new things to appreciate about a situation. Others may see what you don't and may help you view the job in a new way. Challenge yourself to add one thing to the list every day.

» **Make a change.** If you don't like it, change it! If you don't like your cubicle, or if standing all day is causing you physical discomfort, talk to your boss or supervisor to see whether you can change the situation. Maybe you can personalize your workspace with family pictures or some plants to create a space you want to come to every day. Small changes can lead to big changes.

>> **Find inspiration.** Find a way to be inspired by your job. Do you really know the story behind your company? Revisit the mission and vision statements. Help others advance in the workplace. Be the inspiration and change that you want to see. Use your downtime productively to improve the work environment for others and yourself. Identify things you have in common with your co-workers and do those things together to improve the workspace.

>> **Get involved.** Volunteer to help with company events, arrange the office, or decorate the common area. Not only will you be proud of yourself for stepping up, but you may also end up inspiring your co-workers to join you!

>> **Find joy where you are and in what you do.** Some aspects of the job you have are out of your control. Focus on what you can control — your attitude, your contribution, and your commitment to excellence — instead of fretting over the things you can't. Staying focused on the things in your circle of influence helps you avoid wasting your energy and positivity on things for which you have no control over.

Offsetting others' negativity with your positivity

Okay, now I get personal. Although you can do things to try to improve the passion potential of a workplace or a job (see the preceding section), the situation can get a little sticky sometimes when you're dealing with negative co-workers and their less-than-positive effect on the work environment.

You know the type: the constant cynic, the office rain cloud, the *that will never work* meeting downer, the *what's wrong with the way things have always been* person. Every company has them all the way from the very top to the very bottom. If you have a co-worker like this, you may feel as if you're working every day with Eeyore, the perennially depressed naysayer donkey from Winnie the Pooh.

So what can you do when you're forced to share office or life space with a rain cloud?

You have two attitude choices — positive or negative — and both can be very powerful in the workplace and with people in other negative situations. A positive attitude — that is, positive speech, reactions, and actions on your part — can help build a successful culture of unity and teamwork that creates outstanding results for both you and your teammates.

Is it easy? Not always. But you know what they say: Nothing worth having comes easy. With practice, though, learning to react with positivity to negative co-workers can become more automatic. Being positive is a feeling you choose first on the inside before you choose to show it on the outside, and when you make that choice often enough, it becomes second nature, even it if doesn't happen overnight.

Change your thoughts and you change your world.

—NORMAN VINCENT PEALE

Developing a Positive Attitude from the Inside Out

Cultivating a positive attitude first on the inside is important because, whether you know it or not, what you show on the outside reflects what's going on inside. Sure, you can pretend that all is well for a while, and you can hide negative thoughts from some of the people some of the time, but eventually your inner self is going to give you away.

In the following sections, I explain how to develop a positive attitude. You can cultivate a positive attitude in several ways, so if one doesn't work for you, try something else. After you have a good start on being positive, see whether some of the other methods work for you.

Finding simple ways to nurture a positive attitude

Your positive attitude starts in your mind. People and external circumstances may influence your attitude, but for the most part, developing and maintaining a positive attitude starts with you. Cultivating your inner positivity and nurturing it when needed are also up to you.

Yep, positive attitudes need tender loving care. Here are a few helpful tips for encouraging your positive attitude:

>> **Take time for yourself.** Replenishing your positive energy reserve is important. You can't give what you don't have. Take time each day to check your inner positivity gauge. If it needs a fill-up, go for a walk, read a book, or do something special for yourself.

>> **Set goals.** Create small, achievable daily goals for yourself, such as making your bed, working out, or putting your clothes in the laundry hamper instead of dropping them on the floor. Achieving small goals gives you a sense of accomplishment, which contributes to having a positive outlook on your life.

>> **Celebrate small wins.** A win is a win, no matter the size, and they're all worth celebrating. Make a big deal out of every small win. Be your own cheerleader. Small daily wins can set the positivity stage for big career and life wins down the road.

>> **Smile!** Smiling is a guaranteed way to nurture and cultivate positive feelings. When you smile, a chemical reaction happens in your brain that actually helps reduce stress. These chemicals, known as *endorphins*, contain serotonin (which acts as an antidepressant) and dopamine (which enhances motivation, movement, mood, sleep, and behavior management).

Challenging yourself

Okay, here's the single most important concept I want to get across in this chapter: Everyone faces challenges. That's just a part of life. Those challenges you face each day don't decide your future, though. What matters most — both professionally and personally — is how you choose to face these challenges.

For example, one of your current challenges may be getting through this book. You can probably come up with all kinds of excuses and reasons why you can't do it. Here's where your attitude comes in and changes everything.

You can tell yourself that the information contained in this book is good for you — that it's going to help you get a job, keep that job, and improve your life. Or you can tell yourself you don't have time, and reading the book doesn't really matter because nothing is going to change the course of your life. One way of thinking leads you to future success; the other way has you giving up before you've really begun. Reaching your goals starts with choosing your attitude, and then you've got to dig in and do the work to take you the rest of the way.

Nothing can stop the man with the right mental attitude from achieving his goal; nothing on earth can help the man with the wrong mental attitude.

—THOMAS JEFFERSON

Reversing negative thinking with positive affirmations

The average human has thousands and thousands of thoughts each day. Some researchers believe most of them — perhaps even as many as 80 percent — are negative.

Wow! If you're talking negatively to yourself 80 percent of every day, no wonder you may have found succeeding at work and in life difficult in the past. You've been fighting yourself!

If you do experience a lot of negative self-talk, work on turning that negative trend around. You've got to start talking yourself *up!* Reprogramming your thought process starts with positive affirmations or positive self-talk.

Positive affirmations are positive statements and phrases, specific to you, that can help reverse negative thinking patterns (such as the following) that may be silently sabotaging your career and life without your even knowing it!

>> I can't do it.

>> This will never work.

>> I can't learn that.

>> I'm not management material.

>> I can't afford to go back to school. I can't, I can't, I can't.

These kinds of negative thoughts become self-fulfilling prophecies.

When you replace silent negative thoughts and phrases with a lively and positive inner dialogue — and practice, practice, practice — the world becomes a better and brighter place inside and out.

TIP

Positive affirmations can help turn a negative attitude into a positive attitude — the type of attitude that all employers prefer in those they hire.

WARNING

You may not realize that you're having negative thoughts about yourself and that you may be putting yourself down. But if the words *I can't, won't, shouldn't, couldn't,* or *wouldn't* pop into your mind on a regular basis, or if you hear someone else's voice telling you that you can't, chances are that this inner monologue has been standing in the way of your success.

I'm here to tell you that you can, starting today. The following sections give examples of positive affirmations that can help you begin the process of reprogramming your inner voice to create positive thinking and positive self-talk.

Self-esteem affirmations

Use these positive affirmations for improving your *self-esteem* (how you feel about yourself):

>> I embrace my flaws because I know that nobody is perfect.

>> I don't want to look like anyone but myself.

>> I get better every day in every way.

>> I matter, and what I have to offer this world also matters.

>> I love myself deeply and completely.

Adversity affirmations

When faced with adversity or hard times, reflect on these affirmations:

>> I consider failure to be great feedback.

>> I am confident about solving life's problems successfully.

>> I learn from my challenges and always find ways to overcome them.

>> I recognize that challenges are what make life interesting. Overcoming them is what makes them meaningful.

Affirmations for believing in yourself

Some days, believing that you're on the right track in your career, your relationships, or, heck, even your life as a whole is hard. Use these affirmations for believing in yourself and your bright future:

>> If I can conceive it and believe it, I can achieve it.

>> The future is good, and I look foward to it with hope and happiness.

>> I can do whatever I focus my mind on.

>> I follow my dreams no matter what.

>> I am open to all possibilities.

Affirmations that support a positive attitude

Don't get down when you slip into negative thinking. These positive affirmations can help improve your attitude:

>> I compare myself only to my highest self.

>> I am not trying to fit in because I was born to stand out.

>> I refrain from comparing myself to others.

>> I am who I want to be starting right now.

>> I control my emotions; they don't control me.

Being your own best friend

If negative people have a negative effect on those around them, you may assume that positive people have a positive effect, right? Well, not always. No matter how many positive people you may have around you, the most powerful influence on your most personal thoughts is *you*. The second-most-important message I hope to send in this chapter is the knowledge and understanding that for career and life success, you must become your own very best friend because you and only you are responsible for your life. (I cover the most important takeaway in the earlier section "Challenging yourself.")

When you realize that your success is 100 percent up to you and that you possess every soft skills tool you need to succeed on the job and in life, stop looking for others to blame when things don't go your way, and start looking inside yourself for positive affirmation each day, you're well on your way to a bright future filled with career and life success and satisfaction.

REMEMBER

Successful people live by the creed "I can't always choose what happens to me, but I can always choose what happens *in* me."

To choose the right attitude, you have to believe the decision is truly up to you. You choose to be filled with positive energy and a positive outlook, or you don't. It's that simple. So what do you choose?

No matter what may be happening in your workplace or in your personal life, you can always choose to focus on what's right and good. Finding a way to put a positive spin on negative people and situations you face may not be easy at first, but with practice, you eventually find remaining positive in the face of negativity easier. And when you master this — and you can — career and life success follow.

Spinning Up an A+ Attitude

Life acts, and you react. How do you react when faced with change, challenges, failures, and stress? You can't always control what happens in your life, but you can always control how you react to what happens.

That's where the positive attitude spin comes in!

Take this scenario:

> The car in front of you turns suddenly with no signal, causing you to have to slam on your brakes. The birthday cake you're bringing to a co-worker slides off the passenger seat with a sickening thud, causing your heart to sink. You take one hand off the steering wheel so you can let that driver know exactly how you feel about the situation.

The cake is a mess, so what's the positive spin in this situation? You didn't have an accident. Your co-worker will still love you for the birthday thought — because it's the thought that counts — and you may even get a laugh over the state of the cake as you light the candles.

REMEMBER

When you apply a positive attitude to a negative situation, your reactions and your actions reflect that attitude. You may sometimes have difficulty finding a positive spin for a situation, but if you look hard enough, you can identify something. Once again, practice makes perfect.

Exercise: Building an A+ Attitude

Here, I offer an exercise that's designed to help you start to tear down any negative attitude walls that are holding you back from being the best person you can be. The goal is to help you start to build the kind of A+ attitude that can lead to success and happiness both in the workplace and in life, brick by positive brick. As I say often throughout this chapter, it all starts with you.

So grab a pen and get ready to spend a little time getting to know, love, and appreciate yourself a bit better. Discover how to see yourself in a more positive light. Read the following statements and then write your responses to the questions. Feel free to write directly in this book if you choose! (If you have a physical book, that is; if you're reading electronically, maybe consider a separate sheet of paper.)

>> **Love yourself, believe in yourself, and nurture yourself.**

Name all the good things about you.

_____

_____

What's the most recent thing you did to build yourself up or nurture yourself?

_____

_____

Put your attitude to work for you!

Create your own happy file by journaling your progress once a week, and pull it out when you need a reminder that no matter what you do or where you go, you always have you. Be your own biggest fan. As I note earlier in the chapter, celebrating small wins is crucial because they remind you that you're on the right path.

>> **Demonstrate the right attitude and use the healing power of positive emotions.**

How do I rate my personal attitude?

_____

_____

How do I rate my self-esteem?

_____

_____

Am I positive in my daily interactions with people and co-workers?

_____

_____

Put your attitude to work for you!

Give yourself a positive attitude checkup once a month and make adjustments if necessary.

>> **Establish a value system that has high standards of excellence, relates to your goals, and allows you to accomplish your priorities.**

What do you value?

_____

_____

What values were passed to you that you want to hold onto?

_____

_____

Put your attitude to work for you!

When faced with adversity or challenges, stop and reflect on your values and use them to help you move ahead with your goals.

» **Have all the fun you can on this trip called life.**

What are you doing when you're having fun?

_____

_____

When was the last time you had so much fun? What were you doing?

_____

_____

Put your attitude to work for you!

Look up an old friend. Make a phone call. Write a letter. Visit if you can. Go shopping with your inner child. Spend five or ten dollars on something you usually wouldn't buy for yourself. Watch or read something that makes you laugh out loud.

» **Give as good as you get.**

What have I done recently for someone without expecting anything in return?

_____

_____

What would my best friend say about me?

_____

_____

How can I give more to my co-workers and guests?

_____

_____

Put your attitude to work for you!

Make random acts of kindness — for those you do and don't know — a regular part of your life. The first time you experience all the feels and thanks that come your way, you'll discover that giving really is better than receiving!

REMEMBER

Attitude is everything. And you have everything you need to choose, create, and take a positive attitude with you to work each and every day. You can choose to bring it home with you, too, and share it with the people in your life. They'll see the positive change in you and start to change as well. Win. Win. Win.

Looking at Real-Life Scenarios: A Ho-Hum Attitude Versus a Positive Attitude

Compare the following two anecdotes about two employees who have worked for a company for a similar amount of time but who have very different attitudes.

>> **Getting it wrong:** Daniel's been working for the same company for three years. He hasn't been promoted, but he hasn't been demoted. His day-to-day, on-the-job attitude is the same today as it was yesterday and the day before that: *I show up on time (most of the time). I do what I was hired to do. I mind my own business. I don't ask for help and I don't offer help. I just put my head down and do my job.* At the end of every employee evaluation, Daniel's first and only question to his supervisor is "What more do you want from me?"

>> **Getting it right:** Cheryl was hired at the same company the very same week. She's been promoted three times in three years. She's now a team leader and on her way to making supervisor. Her day-to-day, on-the-job attitude is the same today as it was yesterday and the day before that: *I love my job. I love this company. I love learning new things and being given new responsibilities. I'm happy to show up a few minutes early and stay a few minutes late if that's what's necessary to get the job done right.* At the end of every employee evaluation, Cheryl's first and only question is "What more can I do for you?"

VOICES OF INDUSTRY

Jim Link

Chief Human Resource Officer

Society for Human Resource Management

The Society for Human Resource Management (SHRM) creates better workplaces where employers and employees thrive together. As the voice of all things work, workers, and the workplace, SHRM is the foremost expert, organizer, and thought leader on issues impacting today's evolving workplaces. More than 95 percent of Fortune 500 companies rely on SHRM to be their go-to resource for all things work and their business partner in creating next-generation workplaces. With 300,000+ HR and business executive members in 165 countries, SHRM impacts the lives of more than 115 million workers and families globally.

Without question, soft skills give career durability and are highly transferable. The workplace has many hard skills, yet companies gain as much of an advantage by embracing individuals with soft skills as they do those with technical skills. Soft skills such as critical thinking, adaptability and resilience, self-motivation, persuasive communication, organizational skills, innovation, leadership, and interpersonal skills are becoming increasingly critical to the culture of organizations and can be applied to any job.

An organization with leaders who recognize the soft skills in their staff create a culture where employees are more inclined to stay and thrive. Remote working has created a new normal; therefore, it's important to know which soft skills are key for effective remote work and how managers can best identify and bring out those skills in their staff members as they carry out their work remotely. For example, two vital soft skills for working remotely are the ability to be adaptable and resourceful when there is no IT support or to be self-motivated to work alone and without distraction.

Employees should look at successful colleagues around them and identify if there are certain soft skills they possess that align with your company's priorities and can be modeled for personal growth. Online learning, coaching, mentoring, and interactive workshops are great platforms and opportunities for employees to hone their soft skills while on the job. It is beneficial for companies to evaluate the impact of soft-skills training and tie them to their companies' end of year performance plans and key metrics.

If you are in the job market, highlight your soft skills! Soft skills are key to business operations and can give you an advantage over less-experienced candidates.

Chapter 3

Cultivating Top-Notch Character Traits

Attitude is who you are. Character is what you are.

Attitude and character are the foundation of the ten soft skills essential to career and life success. Attitude is *who* you show the world. Character is *what* you show the world. Together, they create the whole you — all you can be and all you can do!

Just like your attitude (which we discuss in Chapter 2), the character you choose to exhibit is 100 percent up to you. You can have positive and negative character traits, just as you can have positive and negative aspects of your attitude. That's why these two 21st-century soft skills go hand-in-hand in the workplace and in life (and in this book).

In this chapter, I emphasize the importance of understanding what constitutes good character and explain how to cultivate positive character traits on your journey up the ladder of career and life success.

Defining Character

Have you ever heard someone say, "so-and-so has good character"? You may have also heard the phrase "that person is quite the character." The difference between the two is massive. Someone who has good character is basically a good person. Loyal, dependable, responsible, trustworthy, kind — just an all-around good person. When someone is quite the character, the phrase comes with a grin and/or an eyeroll, and the speaker usually means that the person has some personality traits that are, well, less than desirable. A person who is quite the character can also have good character, but of the two, having good character is more important.

For succeeding in the workplace, your *character* — the distinctive qualities that describe how you feel, think, and act — can make or break you. Luckily, your character, like your attitude (refer to Chapter 2), is something you can choose *and* change.

Doing the right thing

Character, simply put, is the way you respond to situations at work and in life. Positive personality traits such as honesty, courage, integrity, and loyalty are at the core of good character. Good character involves a person's ability and dependability to consistently make good choices and avoid those that aren't so good.

REMEMBER

People with good character choose to do the right thing because they simply believe it's the right thing to do, not because someone is tracking what they do or they expect a reward for their actions.

Does this description sound like you? I hope so! But if sometimes you don't do the right thing, the good news is that you can choose to work on improving your character starting today. The rest of this chapter provides information about the best character traits and explains how you can develop a character that people respect and admire.

TIP

Imagine your character as an internal compass that guides you to act and to react the way you do to people and situations. Right or wrong, positive or negative, good or bad, win or lose, your character makes every choice in every situation every day. Based on your values, opinions, and beliefs, you can use your inner compass to help guide you to career and life success. You just have to point yourself in the right direction!

Stepping on the character scale

On a scale from 1 to 5 (with 1 being not like you at all and 5 being exactly like you), how would you rate the current state of your character? Read the following statements and give yourself a score that best describes you today.

I'm kind and care about others.				
1	2	3	4	5

I accept responsibility for my choices.				
1	2	3	4	5

I'm honest and trustworthy.				
1	2	3	4	5

I treat others with respect.				
1	2	3	4	5

I'm self-disciplined.				
1	2	3	4	5

I have empathy for others.				
1	2	3	4	5

I have courage.				
1	2	3	4	5

I'm able to forgive others and myself.				
1	2	3	4	5

I have integrity.				
1	2	3	4	5

I walk my talk.				
1	2	3	4	5

I'm friendly.				
1	2	3	4	5

I have healthy relationships.				
1	2	3	4	5

So how did you weigh in on the character scale? Are you currently leaning more to the side of weak character (1) or the side of strong character (5)? Maybe you're smack in the middle (3). You're probably strong in some character respects and bit weak in others, and that's perfectly normal!

Being smack in the middle can leave you stuck in the middle when you're pursuing career and life success, so you always have room for improvement. If you want to reach the top, you need to stand out. And if you want to stand out, you need to stand up and build your character.

Putting in the Work to Build Character

Character isn't something that falls into your lap. You have to be personally motivated to build it and develop it for yourself every day in every challenge and situation you find yourself in. You have to practice making good character choices and good character decisions. When you do so on a regular and dependable basis, others take notice, which often leads to personal and professional rewards.

Filling your blank character slate

The reason you have to develop your character is that good character isn't something you're born with. Character isn't an inherited trait, like the color of your eyes or that dimple in your chin is.

Your character cultivation started during childhood when the adults in your life began teaching you right from wrong, how to share, and so on. As you grew older, you began to take over responsibility for your character cultivation, and you demonstrate it each day in the choices you make in your personal and professional life. Every choice you make — good and bad — contributes to the development of your character.

You can spend your life hoping to wake up one morning to discover you suddenly have a good character, but that's not likely to happen spontaneously. Instead, you need to be proactive and choose to develop it day by day through your experiences and interactions with your customers, co-workers, management, and the people you interact with outside of work.

REMEMBER

Your character is your personal motivation to act the way you do. It comes from the inside and defines what kind of person you are.

Making the best of challenging situations

Developing a good character can be harder than it sounds. As the old saying goes, if it were easy, everyone would do it. The truth is that you go through the most character growth when things heat up and you have to dig deep within yourself to bring forth your good character. You cultivate your good character when you're challenged, and the growth doesn't happen by surviving the hard times. The way you respond when the going gets tough is what defines your character.

Being good and staying on the straight and narrow is easy when things are going your way; the path forward is straight, and following your personal compass is no big deal. But when life gets challenging and you have the choice of a few paths, you have to rely on your character to take you down the right one.

Here's a little story about getting into hot water and how character plays a part in how you approach situations.

> One day, a young woman told her mother that her life and her job were just too hard. She didn't have any friends at work. She wasn't getting anywhere in her career. She was stuck, and she was tired of fighting and struggling to move upward. It seemed as if she'd solve one problem just as a new one cropped up. She just couldn't get ahead and wanted to give up.
>
> The young woman's mother took her into the kitchen and filled three pots with water. She placed three carrots in the first pot, three eggs in the second pot, and some coffee beans in the third pot. She let all three pots come to a boil and left them for 20 minutes without saying a word. Finally, she turned off the stove and moved the three pots to the counter. She fished the carrots out of their pot with a fork and placed them in a bowl. She plucked the eggs out of their pot with tongs and transferred them to another bowl. Finally, she poured the hot coffee into a third bowl.
>
> Turning to the young woman, the mother said, "Tell me what you see."
>
> The young woman replied, "Carrots, eggs, and coffee."
>
> The mother handed her daughter the fork and asked her to pierce the carrots. The daughter noted that they had gotten soft. The mother then asked her daughter to take the egg and break it open. After pulling off the shell, the daughter observed the egg was hard boiled. Finally, the mother asked her daughter to smell and then sip the coffee. The daughter smiled as she smelled the coffee's rich aroma. She took a sip. It was delicious. The daughter turned to her mother and asked, "The coffee is good, the egg is hard, and the carrots are soft. I get all that. But what do carrots, eggs, and coffee have to do with my life?"
>
> The mother smiled and explained that the carrots, the eggs, and the coffee had all faced the same adversity — spending 20 minutes in a pot of boiling water — but

each had reacted differently. The carrots went in strong, hard, and unrelenting but came out softened and weak. The eggs were fragile going in, their liquid insides protected by their delicate shells, but they came out hardened and tough. The coffee beans were unique. Sitting in the boiling water hadn't changed them a bit. In fact, the coffee beans had changed the water to turn it into something good and delicious.

"So which one are you?" the mother asked her daughter. "When trials and adversity knock on your door, how do you respond? Are you a carrot, an egg, or a coffee bean? Which one do you want to be? Which one do you choose to be?"

Which character from the story do you think you are today? Are you a carrot that seems strong but wilts in the face of adversity? Are you the egg that starts out fragile and fluid but becomes hard boiled when situations heat up? Or are you the coffee bean that blossoms in hot water and changes bad situations for the better? Don't let challenges break you down or harden you so that your good character isn't on full display. Instead, let your good character traits rise to the surface to help you make the best of a difficult situation.

REMEMBER

How you react to obstacles and difficulty on the job and in life is a measure of your character. Striving each day to develop desirable character traits that not only help you perform your job to the best of your ability but also *help you help others* be the best they can be is important.

CHARACTER VERSUS REPUTATION

Character is like a tree and reputation like its shadow. The shadow is what we think of it; the tree is the real thing.
—ABRAHAM LINCOLN

Don't confuse character with reputation. Your reputation is what others think and say about you based on their observations of you. Your character is who you truly are on the inside and how you demonstrate it on the outside.

When a person has good character, a good reputation will follow. However, gaining a good reputation shouldn't be the driving force behind having good character. Having good character is important.

Your character is the magic ingredient that makes you uniquely you. Your character — not your reputation — ultimately determines your level of career and life success. Each person has the ability and the potential to develop and strengthen their character and climb the personal and professional ladder all the way to the top.

Grasping the Essence of Character

Ability can help you get you to the top, but character is what keeps you there.

The clarity of your convictions, the choices you make, and the promises you keep reveal the essence of your character. What you say and do defines who you are and what you are. Cultivating good character traits can work wonders for your career and life success, and negative character traits can be absolutely devasting, as I discuss in the following sections.

Employing positive character traits

Every company expects its employees to work together to achieve the organization's objectives. To succeed individually within your company and to help it succeed as a whole, you need to strive each day to develop desirable and positive character traits that help you perform to the best of your ability. The list of positive character traits is long, but here's a look at what I consider to be the top five:

>> **Honesty:** If you prove to be an honest employee, you're well on your way to success within your organization. Don't lie, cheat, or steal. Be reliable by doing what you say you're going to do. Show your co-workers they can count on you.

>> **Responsibility:** You demonstrate responsibility when you're motivated to accomplish your goals. Do what you're supposed to do when you say you're going to do it. Always do your best. Use self-control. Be self-disciplined. Think before you act, and consider the consequences. Be accountable for the choices you make.

>> **Respect:** Respect from others gives you a sense of dignity and builds your self-esteem and self-confidence. How can you return the favor? Treat others with respect and be considerate of their feelings. Follow the Golden Rule. Be tolerant of differences. Use nice manners and language. Deal peacefully with anger, insults, and disagreements.

>> **Initiative:** Successful people do even things that they don't want to do. They also see where action is needed and get the ball rolling to fill that hole. A person who does these things has *initiative*. Taking initiative means doing what you don't want to do because you know if you do it anyway you're going to get ahead in your career and life. Do what you're supposed to do and look for gaps where other people aren't doing what's needed, and then take the opportunity to step up in those areas, too.

>> **Loyalty:** People with good character are loyal to their employers, their families, and their communities. Loyal people are trustworthy. They can be counted on no matter what. In turn, loyal people have lots of friends to rely on, and loyal employees often get rewarded and promoted.

Steering clear of negative character traits

The dark side of character: those character traits that are negative. Although I want to accentuate the positive, knowing what your good character traits are up against is always wise.

Here's a look at our top five negative character traits:

>> **Arrogance:** Arrogant people want what they want when they want it. It's their way or the highway. They take the low road.

>> **Rudeness:** Rude people treat the rest of the world with zero respect. They don't listen, and they don't care. They lack basic decency and manners. They don't have many friends or great career prospects.

>> **Insensitivity:** Insensitive people don't have a clue about what's going on with the people around them at work and in life because they're completely and totally concerned only with themselves. Insensitivity is the opposite of empathy (which isn't on our top five list of good character traits but is still important).

>> **Apathy:** Apathetic people (yawn) just don't care. They simply can't be bothered. Most of the time they prefer to be left alone. And most of the time, they are.

>> **Anger:** Angry people stomp around in a haze of negativity, using mean and hurtful language that puts up walls between them and personal and professional happiness and success.

REMEMBER

You may have heard this quotation, usually attributed to Maya Angelou: "People will forget what you said, people will forget what you did, but people will never forget how you made them feel." Strive to always make those around you feel good. What you put forth will be reflected back to you.

Recognizing How to Make Character Count

Do you have the positive character traits you need to succeed in your career and life? Or could your character use a little work? (Refer to the "Grasping the Essence of Character" section earlier in the chapter to determine whether you're exhibiting positive or negative character traits.) Whether you need to do a little work or a lot, remember that everyone always has room for character improvement. The more positive character traits you have and portray, the more career and life success and happiness you achieve. And practice makes perfect.

As I note in the earlier section "Defining Character," some people have good character, and some simply are characters. Good character makes one memorable. People with good character make lasting impressions on their family, friends, and co-workers. People who are characters, on the other hand, are more flash-in-the-pan personalities. They get their proverbial 15 minutes of fame and then often are soon forgotten. The following two-part exercise helps you identify the difference between having character and being a character.

>> Part one: Come up with answers (without searching the Internet) for each of the following items:

1. Name the five wealthiest people in the world.

2. Name the last five Olympic 100-meter sprint gold medalists.

3. Name the last five winners of the Miss Universe contest.

4. Name ten people who have won the Nobel Prize.

5. Name the last half dozen Academy Award winners for best actor or actress.

How did you do? If you came up empty, don't sweat it. That's the whole point. Sure, once upon a time all these people were the best in their fields and almost everyone knew their names. But fame is fleeting. Achievements are forgotten, and accolades and certificates are buried with their owners. These types of people are characters on the world stage, and they may have also had character, but that's not what stood out about them.

>> Part two: Come up with answers for these items:

1. Name a few teachers who aided your journey through school.

2. Name three friends who have helped you through a difficult time.

3. Name five people who have taught you something worthwhile.

4. Name a few people who made you feel appreciated and special.

5. Name five people you enjoy spending time with.

Part two was much easier, yes? Names were probably popping up in your head like popcorn because, unlike the people on the first list, these people mean something to you. They and their good character have had a positive impact on your life. The people on the first list are characters, but the people on your second list have character. That's why they're so easy to name. That's why they're so memorable.

TIP

Want to show up on somebody's part-two list? Then keep the following sentiment attributed to Frank Outlaw in mind:

>> Watch your thoughts; they become words.

>> Watch your words; they become actions.

GOOD CHARACTER RETAINS ITS VALUE

A well-known speaker started off a seminar by showing his 200-member audience a $20 bill and asking, "Who would like this $20 bill?" Hands started popping up all over the auditorium.

The speaker then crumpled the bill in his hand and asked, "Who still wants it?" The hands remained in the air. He finally dropped it, ground it into the floor with his shoe, and then reached down and picked up the now-crushed and dirty money. "Now who still wants it?" The hands still remained in the air.

The speaker smiled and said, "My friends, we have all learned a very valuable lesson. No matter what I did to this piece of money, you still wanted it because, even crumpled and dirty, the bill did not decrease one cent in value. It was still worth $20."

The character moral of this story is that everyone encounters times in life when they find themselves dropped, crumpled, and ground into the dirt by the decisions they make and the challenges that come their way. And though they may feel at the time that they're worthless, no matter what happens, if they maintain their good character, remain positive, and look to their inner compass, they'll never lose their value.

Your life worth comes not from who you may know or what you may achieve but from who you are.

>> Watch your actions; they become habits.

>> Watch your habits; they become character.

>> Watch your character, for it becomes your destiny.

Looking at Real-Life Scenarios: Character in action

A popular clothing store has just hired two new assistant manager trainees. On paper, these two new hires are equal in just about every way. They've both worked in the retail industry for three years. They both worked their way up from sales positions. On their first day on the new job, they're both scheduled to arrive at the store at 9 a.m., an hour before opening.

>> **Getting it wrong:** Assistant manager trainee number one arrives right on time and gets right down to what they believe is assistant manager business. They boss the salespeople around, bark orders, and don't lift a finger to get the store ready for the new business day. And why should they? They're in management now. They've paid their dues on the floor. They've folded their share of T-shirts; they've hung up more dresses than they can count. This moment is their time to shine. The sales team members obey the orders of their new assistant manager, but they do so with shared eyerolls and shaking heads. One team member whispers, "Would you get a load of *that* character?"

>> **Getting it right:** Assistant manager trainee number two also arrives right on time and also gets right down to what they believe is assistant manager business. They jump right into work with the team members, folding shirts, hanging dresses, and doing whatever's necessary to get the store ready for the new business day. They don't need to shine. The store needs to shine. That's their job as assistant manager. They work side by side with their co-workers, encouraging them and complimenting their hard work. When the store opens at 10 a.m., they're polite to every customer who walks through the door, and they're happy to pitch right in when things get busy on the floor.

When the store closes for the day and the team members head off for a pizza and some after-work fun, guess who gets invited to join them. Assistant manager trainee one or two? Do they invite the character or the person *with* character?

Most likely, they'll pick the latter. It's simple and true: Character counts! So like the second assistant manager trainee, make your character count for you every single day in every single way in every single career and life situation you encounter.

VOICES OF INDUSTRY

Bruce Gardner

Vice President, Member Services

Business-Higher Education Forum

Bruce is a graduate of Brown University who spent more than 30 years with IBM, a global leading technology provider, where he worked in sales with clients of all sizes and managed people in various sales and executive positions. After retiring from IBM, he

(continued)

(continued)

went to work for Business-Higher Education Forum (BHEF), a nonprofit member organization comprised of chief executive officers (CEOs) in business and university presidents. This senior group is focused on identifying talent pathways and emerging skills necessary for students to be successful in an ever-changing workplace. Bruce also spent nine years as an elected school board member and served four times as chair, interviewed prospective students for his alma mater, and coached countless youth sports teams.

It could be argued that soft skills have been the number-one most important factor in my success in life — both career and personal.

There's an old saying in sales: "People buy from people they like." IBM believed in "establishing rapport" and listening to the customer before ever selling them something that could help them. IBM's "Basic Beliefs" included responsibility and care for the individual. These soft skill practices and values — along with IBM's professional look, trustworthy reputation, and commitment to the client's success — helped it become a world-class company.

"People buy from people they like" transcends beyond sales to everyday life. People also want to be around people they like, and that's usually people who communicate easily, have a positive attitude, follow through on their commitments, and have a trusted character. Maybe not everything you need to know you learned in kindergarten, as the saying goes, but it sure lays a pretty solid foundation.

Certainly, in today's technology-based world, it helps to have some depth in one's skills. The STEM focus, all the K-12 learning standards, being a "T-shaped learner" (knowledgeable across an array of subjects but particularly deep in one), an ability to code or use data analytics to identify and predict patterns — all of these will help increase one's employability.

But soft skills open the doors to opportunity. I've been fortunate to serve in numerous leadership capacities. These have allowed me to help provide clients with service; to lead school systems, neighborhood associations, and sports teams; to oversee a 425-member golf club; and to serve my church. No one cared what my degree was, but they saw my willingness to volunteer, work hard for the greater good of others, listen to multiple opinions, form a vision, and articulate the rationale behind ideas. I believe the world needs more soft skills today.

2

Going Even Further with Soft Skills

Understand the three *V*s of communication.

Respect diversity and model inclusion by embracing people's differences.

Set the stage to make a good impression through your appearance and etiquette.

Manage your time to be efficient and productive.

Build a strong sense of teamwork and manage conflict among teammates.

Develop your ability to ask questions, think critically and independently, and solve problems.

Put the ten work-ethic traits to use.

Enhance your leadership skills and recognize different types of leaders.

IN THIS CHAPTER

» Understanding the importance of good communication skills

» Using the three Vs of interpersonal communication

» Identifying the ten listening blocks that break down communication

» Communicating with strong verbal and nonverbal messages

Chapter 4

Being Clear with Interpersonal Communication

I n this chapter, I talk about, well, talking. But we also talk about listening, which is one of the most important soft skills you can acquire in pursuing work and life success. Most importantly, I talk about *connecting.*

It's a fact: People who are able to truly connect with others . . . You can make positive connections with your co-workers, managers, friends, and family members in all kinds of ways, and they all include the ability to communicate clearly and effectively.

Making all the Right Connections

Are you the kind of communicator that gets as good as you give? A good communicator really listens when someone is talking by concentrating on the speaker's words and voice inflections. A good communicator also watches to see what the speaker isn't saying in actual words but is clearly conveying with their body language. Are you an engaged listener, or are you the kind of communicator who's so busy thinking about your reply — about what *you* want to say — that your connections with others are pretty much broken before they've even begun?

Even reading requires communication and connection. Be honest: Are you really connecting to what you're reading right now?

TIP

Some people find that reading aloud helps them connect better with the material — that's why parents and teachers read aloud to children — so if you learn better when listening, then by all means, be proud and read aloud! (Unless you happen to be in a public library, where doing so may get you shushed!)

REMEMBER

Many people underestimate the importance of effective interpersonal communication. It's just talking, right? Well, not quite. Surveys show that having and demonstrating strong, positive, and effective communication skills can take a person from good to great both personally and professionally.

Stepping on the Communication Scale

Interpersonal communication takes place when you're talking face-to-face with a student, a colleague, a supervisor, a friend, a family member, or even a stranger. On a scale of 1 to 5, how you would you rate your interpersonal communication skills?

Now that you've estimated how good your skills are, use the following soft skills communication scale to see how you really weigh in. Read each of the following statements and choose your response on a scale from 1 to 5 (with 1 being not like you at all and 5 being exactly like you). Remember to be honest. This assessment isn't a test. It's a starting point to becoming the best communicator you can be.

I tend to let my actions speak louder than my words.				
1	2	3	4	5
People trust my words and consider me to be honest.				
1	2	3	4	5
When talking to people, I pay attention to their body language.				
1	2	3	4	5
I can tell when someone doesn't understand what I'm saying.				
1	2	3	4	5

I try not to think about what I'm going to say next when someone is talking to me.				
1	2	3	4	5
I try not to answer questions with just a "yes" or a "no."				
1	2	3	4	5
I realize that for good communication, listening is just as important as talking.				
1	2	3	4	5
If I don't understand someone, I try to ask questions to clarify what they are saying.				
1	2	3	4	5
I find it easy to see things from someone else's point of view.				
1	2	3	4	5
I manage to express my ideas clearly.				
1	2	3	4	5

If your score falls between 38 and 45 points, you're an upfront, confident interpersonal communicator! Way to go! Keep working to further enhance your interpersonal communication skills.

If your score is in the 26 to 37 range, you're tipping the scale in the right interpersonal direction. You still have some developing and practicing to do before you're completely confident in face-to-face communication situations, but you can do it. Keep going!

If your score is 25 or less, you're challenged when faced with upfront and personal communication, both with yourself and others. But have no fear! I commend your honesty, and I know with a little courage and determination you can meet and beat the challenge!

Getting Connected

Effective *interpersonal communication* is the process by which people exchange information, feelings, and intention through active listening and verbal and non-verbal messages. To successfully communicate with others both at work and in life, you must first be able to connect with them. I want to repeat that because it's so important: Connect first. Communicate second.

That means you have to listen. Listen first and talk second. Wait. What? Who does that? People with effective interpersonal communication skills, that's who.

REMEMBER

Interpersonal communication is all about making connections; it focuses on building meaningful relationships.

Listening first, talking second

Human beings have one mouth and two ears for a reason: so I would listen twice as much as I speak. Sadly, that's not the way it works most of the time. Our ears may work perfectly well, and we may *hear* just fine. The problem is I don't put them to work often enough. I don't really *listen*.

REMEMBER

The difference between hearing and listening is important. *Hearing* is what happens when you receive the auditory stimulus of someone else speaking, and you go through motions of listening: nodding your head and/or changing your expressions while your mind and/or your fingers are busy doing something else. *Listening* is what happens when you receive the auditory stimulus but you also connect and communicate with your entire person and keep your mind focused on the message the speaker is conveying. Listening tells the person speaking to you, "I'm here, front and center, and I hear you. I get it."

Framing the walls of disconnection

REMEMBER

As I discuss in the preceding section, making a connection with someone when you're hearing but not listening is hard. If you're doing something other than focusing on the conversation happening right in front of you — for example, thinking about what you want for lunch or what you want to do this weekend — rather than building an effective relationship, you're erecting a wall of disconnection blocks that keeps you from really communicating and connecting.

We need to talk about those pesky disconnection blocks and how people build walls with them. As they say, knowledge is power. (I show you lots of positive ways you can break down disconnect walls in the "Becoming a Communication Champion" section later in the chapter.)

The following are common disconnection blocks that get in the way of successful communication. Not all of them come into play in every personal and professional communication situation, but being aware of them when communicating with others at work and in life is essential. Think about your listening skills as you review each block.

>> **Rehearsing:** When someone is talking and you're busy silently rehearsing or planning your own reply, you're breaking your listening concentration and blocking the opportunity for a real connection.

>> **Judging:** If you're focused on how the person you're communicating with is dressed or how they look or speak, you can prejudge the speaker, dismiss their idea as unimportant or uninformed, and put up a disconnect block.

>> **Identifying:** When you're listening to someone tell a story but are so occupied thinking about your own experience that you launch into your own story before the person is finished telling theirs, you may lose sight of what the other person was trying to communicate, and you definitely miss the connection.

>> **Advising:** If you try to offer advice before a person has finished explaining a situation, you may not fully understand the situation.

>> **Sparring:** If you're focused on disagreeing with what someone is saying, you're probably not giving that person an honest chance to fully express their thoughts.

>> **Put-downs:** When you use sarcastic comments to put down someone's point of view, you can draw that person into an argumentative conversation in which neither of you hears a word the other says. The result: *dis*-connection.

>> **Being right:** If you're so intent on proving your point or adamantly refusing to admit to any wrongdoing, you may end up twisting the facts, shouting, and making excuses. These actions may confuse and upset both you and the person you're talking to.

>> **Derailing:** When you suddenly change the subject while someone is talking or joke about what they're saying, you're likely to weaken that speaker's trust in both you and your ability to show understanding.

>> **Smoothing over:** When you'll do anything to avoid conflict or often choose to agree with what someone is saying simply because you want others to like you, you may appear to be supportive. However, never expressing a personal point of view is an obvious signal that you aren't fully engaged in the conversation.

>> **Daydreaming:** If you tune out while someone is talking to you and let your mind wander from random thought to random thought, you've completely disconnected from the conversation.

TIP

Listen with curiosity. Speak with honesty. Act with integrity. The greatest problem with communication is that people don't listen to understand. They listen to reply. When you listen with curiosity, you don't listen with the intent to reply. You listen for what's behind the words.

Completing the Connection with the Three Vs

Effective interpersonal communication is less about how well you're able to converse and more about how well you're able to be understood. Your ability to make that oh-so-important connection comes into play. (Check out the earlier section "Getting Connected" for more on that topic.)

Connecting and communicating effectively with others is as easy as the three Vs: the *visual*, the *vocal*, and the *verbal* components of a conversation. The three Vs represent how much information you give and receive when you communicate with others. When you incorporate all three Vs into your interpersonal communication skill-set, your personal and professional interactions can be amazingly easy, effective, and successful.

REMEMBER

To create and cultivate effective interpersonal communication skills and to make a 100 percent genuine connection with another person, you must communicate with your entire being: your ears, your eyes, your words, and your heart!

Doing the math

Most people probably think "verbal" is the most important of the three Vs for effective communication. After all, if you're not saying anything, how can you possibly communicate?

The real math tells a different story:

>> *Visual interpersonal communication* (your body language) controls 55 percent of all interpersonal communication. Talk about actions speaking louder than words!

>> *Vocal interpersonal communication* (the tone, quality, and rate of your speaking voice) controls 38 percent of all interpersonal communication.

>> *Verbal interpersonal communication* (the actual words spoken) controls only 7 percent of all interpersonal communication.

Surprise, surprise. On the interpersonal communication importance scale, verbal skills come in dead last. Yep. You read that right.

Ninety-three percent of all information given and received in every single conversation is directly related to nonverbal communication skills, proving beyond a shadow of a doubt that for effective and successful communicators, *how* you say it counts more than *what* you say.

Lucky for you, you only need to sharpen two tools to cultivate your nonverbal communication skills, and you already have both: your eyes and your ears. When you connect with your ears, you give every conversation a 38 percent interpersonal communication boost. Add in your eyes, and you get an extra 55 percent of successful interpersonal communication and connection power.

Speaking from the heart

Because nonverbal communication elements make up 93 percent of each personal connection (as I explain in the preceding section), finding a way to make the verbal element — the 7 percent — really, really count is crucial. Every single word matters. And to make the words matter, you also have to connect with your heart by speaking with sincerity and honesty. The ability to share and care matters as much in interpersonal communication as it does with your attitude (refer to Chapter 2) and character (Chapter 3).

Becoming a Communication Champion

This section is (I think) the fun part. Here I show you how to break down your detrimental work and life disconnection walls and build a brand-new set of interpersonal communication skills to help you emerge as an excellent communicator visually, vocally, and verbally. (You can read more about those components of communication in the earlier section "Completing the Connection with the Three Vs.")

Talking about body language

Four factors figure into becoming a champion visual communicator: eye contact, posture, gesturing, and facial expression. Each aspect contributes to making contact and generating connection when you're interacting with others.

>> **Eye contact:** You probably know what talking to someone whose eyes are constantly moving and focusing on everything but you feels like. The person scans the room, looks over your shoulder or down at their phone, or gazes out the window. It's like trying to hit a moving target!

Eye contact is perhaps the most powerful form of nonverbal communication. When you make eye contact with the person you're communicating with, you're saying, "I'm interested in you. I'm paying attention to you. I want to connect with you!"

Making eye contact is the ultimate compliment to the person you're communicating with; it shows that you're really listening and that what they're saying is important to you. So keep your face forward and your eyes on the prize.

TIP

Although I do consider eye contact an important component of good communication, I also recognize that for some people, eye contact is a challenge because it's uncomfortable or may be culturally inappropriate. If this applies to you, you may want to consider being forthright with people you're speaking to. Saying something such as, "Please know that while I may not always be making eye contact with you, you have my total attention. I actually absorb information better when I allow my eyes to take in my full environment" lets the other person know that you respect what they're saying and that you're listening attentively even though you're looking elsewhere.

>> **Posture:** When you slouch in your chair or stand or walk with your shoulders rounded, your body sends a message that you're tired, unassertive, or lazy. Champion communicators carry themselves with ease and confidence. This mindset means standing up straight with your shoulders back in a relaxed manner. If you carry and present yourself as though you feel good about yourself, others get the message loud and clear. Stand tall, walk the walk, and let your body do the positive talking.

>> **Gesturing:** *Gestures* include moving your hands, arms, shoulders, and even your head as you speak to help explain or support your message. They add information and variety to a conversation, and you can tell a lot about a speaker by watching their gestures closely. People can reveal nervousness by repeated movements such as swinging or tapping their feet or drumming their fingers.

TIP

Be careful to consider the gesture in the context of the situation, though. For example, one of the most common conversational gestures is crossing your arms in front of your chest. This move can indicate anxiety, disagreement, or a desire to self-protect. However, it can also mean a person is just shy or is simply more comfortable in the arms-crossed position. It doesn't necessarily mean that they're closed-off or defiant.

>> **Facial expressions:** The expression on your face reveals a lot about your attitude. By simply watching your facial expressions as you speak, a listener can tell whether you're happy, sad, angry, or confused.

Facial expressions are very natural, but some people avoid using them, preferring to put on a deadpan expression so they don't show emotion. For a listener, talking to a person with a deadpan expression is not only uninteresting but also uncomfortable because it's so unnatural.

REMEMBER

Not all facial expressions are completely reliable. Many people have learned to fake certain facial expressions when they think those are expected. When a speaker's facial expression doesn't match their verbal message, people tend to put more faith in the facial expression than the spoken word.

Raising your voice

In this section, I'm not talking about literally shouting. I just want to cover how you can use your vocal intonation to communicate clearly with other people.

Being a great vocal communicator involves the following four components: variety, speed, volume, and pauses. Get these right and you're good to go!

>> **Variety:** No one likes to listen to a speaker whose voice never changes in tone or inflection. This situation is called speaking in *monotone*. You maybe have seen the clip from *Ferris Bueller's Day Off* in which Ferris's teacher, played by Ben Stein, repeats, "Bueller, Bueller," as he's taking attendance. That teacher is a perfect example of someone who speaks in a monotone. He sounds like he's not interested in or excited about what he's saying. When you speak, use variety in the tone and inflection of your voice to add interest and enthusiasm to the words you speak.

>> **Speed:** You want to talk at a rate that allows those listening to both understand and remember what you're saying. Sometimes, you need to push the slow-mo button, especially if your message includes many details or technical information. On the other hand, if the information isn't technical, you don't want your speaking rate to be too slow, or people may become bored or offended.

>> **Volume:** How you control your volume can enhance or detract from your message. For example, you may want to raise your voice to emphasize a point you're making. However, constantly speaking at top volume can have a negative effect on your audience. At the same time, you don't want to speak so softly that no one can hear you. (Of course, your environment dictates the volume of your voice to some extent. If you're at a concert or a crowded football game, you may have to raise your voice to be heard.)

>> **Pauses:** Vocalized pauses happen when a person interrupts their message with vocal sounds such *um, er,* or *uh* or repeats certain phrases such as "you know" or "like." Vocalized pauses make a speaker sound like they're unsure of themselves, their subject matter, or both, so do your best to not fall into this habit.

Using your words

TIP

Before you jump right in and say whatever pops into your mind, take a step back and make sure you're speaking honestly and from the heart. As I explain throughout the chapter, communication isn't just what you say; it's also how you say it.

Every time you send words out into the world, it's like throwing a boomerang — your words always find their way back to you. As a rule, if you communicate with others positively, you attract kind and positive words in return. Sure, some people never have a kind word to say to anyone, but you don't have to be one of them! Here are ten verbal communication tips to help you become a champ at using your words:

>> **Keep it simple.** The key to being an effective communicator is simplicity. Forget about trying to impress people with big words or complex sentences. If you really want to connect with people, keep your message simple. What's the one main idea you want your listener(s) to remember? Say it simply, in one short sentence. Don't overload your conversation with information.

>> **Use clear, direct words.** Words have power, so use them wisely. Use language your listeners can understand. Talk to them on their level; don't talk over their heads, but don't talk down to them, either. It's called relating. Connecting.

>> **See your audience.** Effective communicators focus on their audience when communicating. They understand that you can't effectively communicate without knowing something about the person or people you're talking to.

People believe in great communicators because great communicators believe in people.

REMEMBER

>> **Show the truth.** If your listeners don't believe in you, they won't believe a word you say. You convey credibility in two ways when speaking. First, believe in what you say. Second, live what you say. It's that simple.

>> **Respect your listeners.** Keep your listeners' interests in mind. Let them know how the information helps them and how to apply it. If you're speaking with one individual, use that person's name. Treat your listeners as people who are important to you.

>> **Repeat your main idea.** Before you finish delivering your message, repeat the main idea. Doing so emphasizes the most important part of your message and help your listeners both understand and remember it.

>> **Check for understanding.** After you've delivered your message, ask your listeners whether they need clarification or have any questions. If a listener indicates that your message is unclear, respond with comments such as, "I'm not sure I said that clearly; tell me what you think I said."

>> **Stay on point.** Keep your sentences short and to the point. Don't ramble or make your listeners scramble to follow your train of thought. Your best friends as a communicator are simplicity and clarity.

>> **Refocus your attention.** When speaking, keep your focus on your listeners and not the message you're trying to deliver. You should have that practiced,

perfected, and down pat. When you can keep your focus on the audience and off yourself, you're a better and more effective communicator.

>> **Live your message.** Do you recognize any discrepancies between what you say and what you do? If you're not sure, talk to a few trustworthy people and ask them whether you're living your message — that is, honestly and effectively walking your talk. Receive their comments without defensiveness. Then make changes in your life to be more consistent about what you say and what you show.

The following quote from Mahatma Gandhi perfectly sums up these suggestions:

TIP Keep your thoughts positive because your thoughts become your words. Keep your words positive because your words become your behavior. Keep your behavior positive because your behavior becomes your habit. Keep your habits positive because your habits become your values. Keep your values positive because your values become your destiny.

Looking at Real-Life Scenarios: Understanding the Value of Listening

A restaurant manager has called an employee meeting with their waitstaff. The agenda: how to improve customer service and increase customer loyalty to promote return visits to the restaurant. The manager notified the waitstaff of this meeting two days in advance and told each waitperson to come prepared with ideas to help the restaurant reach its goals. After starting the meeting off with a short inspirational speech, the manager is now listening as each staff member takes a turn presenting their ideas to the team.

>> **Getting it wrong:** Waitperson number one has no idea who or how many of the waitstaff have already spoken, who's speaking now, what has already been said, or what's being said now because they're scribbling furiously on a piece of paper, making a last-minute list of what will turn out to be not-very-original ideas. Result: Not only will waitperson number one look a bit foolish when they present the very same ideas that others have, but their co-workers will also realize waitperson number one hasn't listened to a single word any of them said. They'll lose all respect for that person, who didn't show any to them. On top of all that, the restaurant manager, who has been watching waitperson number one since the meeting started, will decide that a waitperson who can't be bothered to look up and listen to co-workers probably isn't

the most effective front-of-the-house communicator either, and poor waitperson number one may be out of a job.

>> **Getting it right:** Waitperson number two arrived at the meeting fully prepared to speak as well as listen. They comment on each of their co-worker's presentations, compliment them on their ideas, and make their engagement in the conversation perfectly clear to both their co-workers and the restaurant manager. Waitperson number two is fully in command of their visual, vocal, and verbal communication, and their connection skills are high. Result: Their co-workers listen to and support the ideas presented by waitperson number two because they give as good as they got. And a week later, the restaurant manager, still impressed with waitperson number two's ability to effectively and successfully communicate and connect with both co-workers and customers, promotes waitperson number two to the position of assistant manager.

VOICES OF INDUSTRY

Martin Guay

Vice President, Business Development

Stanley Black & Decker

Headquartered in the USA, Stanley Black & Decker is the world's largest tool company operating nearly 50 manufacturing facilities across America and more than 100 world-wide. Guided by its purpose — for those who make the world — the company's more than 60,000 diverse and high-performing employees produce innovative, award-winning power tools, hand tools, storage, digital tool solutions, lifestyle products, outdoor products, engineered fasteners, and other industrial equipment to support the world's makers, creators, tradespeople, and builders. The company's iconic brands include DEWALT, BLACK+DECKER, CRAFTSMAN, STANLEY, Cub Cadet, Hustler, and Troy-Bilt. Recognized for its leadership in environmental, social, and governance (ESG), Stanley Black & Decker strives to be a force for good in support of its communities, employees, customers and other stakeholders.

What is the most important determinant for career success or for someone's organizational efficacy? Debate will revolve around several factors such as education, experience, and technology fluency. They are very significant. Yet without soft skills, career success may not be optimized nor potentially ever achieved.

We live in a world awash in information and concurrent measurements on every facet of human work and human activity. Everything is measured as a data point, an analysis, or a trend. We have become mathematical inputs generating data in our jobs and mathematical outcomes of our efforts in the guise of KPIs, results, and metrics. In many ways, we seem to be factors in multiple algorithms.

Yet is this how value is created in the workforce? Or can other factors become as important at technical inputs and mathematical outputs?

People make the difference. Without the skills and abilities to communicate with people, to collaborate with people, and to create with people, education and experience are not enough to achieve optimal individual and collective success. Soft skills are the glue that binds success together.

Over my career, I have had the chance to lead businesses and to build companies. A mentor early in my career gave me priceless advice. He said, "Hire for behavior and train for skill. Most people hire for skill and fire for behavior." These behaviors are soft skills — communication, respect, transparency, work ethic, team play, and so on. I have used this advice and know it is true. Without soft skills, a new employee's chance of success is challenged.

What you do in business is important, but how you do it is the game changer. Hiring employees with soft skills ensures their success and your organization's success. Soft skills are the foundation of professional success.

IN THIS CHAPTER

» **Understanding the basic components of culture**

» **Welcoming experiences outside the realm of your culture**

» **Recognizing the observable and unseen facets of diversity**

» **Seeing past your conditioning to embrace people's differences**

» **Acknowledging your biases**

Chapter **5**

Respecting Diversity and Developing Cultural Awareness

Each of us shines in a different way, but that doesn't make our light any less bright.

You live in a big wide world filled with all kinds of people, and if you choose not to interact with those who are different from you, you're going to miss a lot of opportunities to enrich your life. The phrase "same old, same old" is true. Same gets old. Consequently, you need to be able to not just tolerate differences among people but genuinely embrace and celebrate them.

In this chapter, you find out how to understand and respect diversity (differences among people), how to recognize how much people share in spite of those differences, and how to become more culturally aware personally and professionally.

Defining Culture

We all smile in the same language.

Each of the world's cultures has its own definition of what's beautiful and what's ugly, what's right and what's wrong, and what's acceptable behavior and what isn't. For example, the way a handshake is delivered in one culture (firm and of short duration) may be completely different than what is expected in another culture (light and prolonged). The culture in which you live influences and guides the way you interpret, think about, feel about, and respond to your personal life experiences and your interactions with others in the workplace and in life, and the same is true of all the people you interact with in the world around you.

Understanding other cultures as well as your own helps you know how to interpret the world. For example, you learn how close to stand to other people, how to greet friends and strangers, when to speak and when to be silent, and how to express your feelings appropriately.

Knowledge of cultural differences influences how you respond to these differences and can help make you aware of hidden prejudices and stereotypes that can be barriers to tolerance, understanding, and good communication. I cover these obstacles in the later section "Saying No to Stereotyping."

REMEMBER

When you care more about what you share with others than what sets you apart and you work to understand, accept, and celebrate differences among the people you know, you contribute to a workplace and a world of positivity and peace.

Delving into dominant cultural patterns

The beliefs and behaviors held by the majority of the people within a particular culture are called *dominant cultural patterns*. Dominant cultural patterns are the beliefs and behaviors you may observe most often when you encounter a person from a particular culture.

REMEMBER

Of course, even the most dominant cultural patterns don't necessarily apply to everyone in that culture.

Often, a society passes down its cultural history or heritage (its beliefs, values, views, and behaviors) from generation to generation. However, a person's perceptions of the world don't develop from culture alone; other elements contribute to the development of individual views and values. Other influences include family, media, religion or spirituality, and government. Culture is dynamic, and as the needs and values of a society change, its cultural patterns also may change.

Stepping Out of Your Cultural Comfort Zone

Imagine not being friends with someone simply because ice cream is the favorite dessert in their culture, and your culture prefers cake. The fact is, if you tried it, you may actually like ice cream (or better yet, ice cream and cake together!)

But because ice cream isn't part of your culture, you're afraid to try it. You're afraid to step out of your culture comfort zone. You're not alone. Your would-be friend is equally afraid to try cake because they're equally unwilling to step out of their cultural comfort zone. Because of those barriers, you may each go your separate ways without knowing what you missed or what you may have been able to create if you had put the treats together!

REMEMBER

The foundational soft skills of attitude and character have an internal focus. Chapters 2 and 3, which cover those two soft skills, could have subtitles of "I Gotta Be Me." Respecting diversity and developing cultural awareness are externally focused soft skills, so we could aptly subtitle this chapter "I Gotta Be We."

Today's world (not to mention today's workplaces, schools, sports teams, and so on) is a rich and wonderful amalgamation of races, religions, cultural beliefs, and customs. In truth, no two people are exactly the same, though they may share certain values and beliefs. To succeed at work and in life, you have to get along with others no matter how much or how little you share in common for things to go along smoothly.

Diving beneath the Diversity Iceberg

Diversity is the inclusion of people of different religions, political orientations, sexual orientations, gender identities, ages, races, ethnicities, socioeconomic statuses, and family structures in a community, group, or organization. Diversity also encompasses differences in cultural backgrounds, values, and ways of life. How you choose to respond to the diversity around you and the cultural differences you encounter every day has a huge impact on your future career and life success. (Head to the earlier section for "Defining Culture" for more on cultural awareness.)

TIP

Think of diversity as being like the iceberg in Figure 5-1. Only the tip of the iceberg sticks out of the water; a lot more of it's under the surface. And the part you can't see is more powerful and important than what lies above. That's why getting below the surface when interacting with others rather than drawing conclusions based only on what you see superficially is crucial.

The same is true of cultural awareness: What you see on the surface almost never tells a person's whole story. Certain aspects or features of culture, such as dress, language, and outward appearance, are visible. But if you look deeper, you discover that many aspects of culture are invisible, meaning they can only be suspected or imagined.

Grab a pen and some paper and try this exercise: The following numbered items are all features of culture. Take a look at the list and see whether you can place each culture feature where it belongs. Make two columns, "Observable aspects" and "Suspected aspects." If you consider a feature observable behavior — something you can see on the outside — write the number in the Observable column. If you consider a feature to be something you can't see, write its number in the Suspected column. *Note:* Many of these items are debatable depending on how you observe and suspect things.

TIP

If you're reading a physical copy of this book, you can even write the observable and suspected numbers above and below the waterline in Figure 5-1 for a more visual reference.

1. Facial expression
2. Religious beliefs
3. Religious rituals
4. Importance of time
5. Paintings
6. Values
7. Literature
8. Child-raising beliefs
9. Concepts of leadership
10. Gestures
11. Holiday customs
12. Concepts of fairness

13. Nature of friendship
14. Notions of modesty
15. Foods
16. Eating habits
17. Concepts of self
18. Work ethic
19. Concepts of beauty
20. Music
21. Styles of dress
22. General worldview
23. Personal space
24. Rules of etiquette

Suspected aspects: 3, 4, 6, 8, 9, 12, 13, 14, 17, 18, 19, 20, 23, 24

Observable aspects: 1, 2, 5, 7, 10, 11, 15, 16, 21, 22

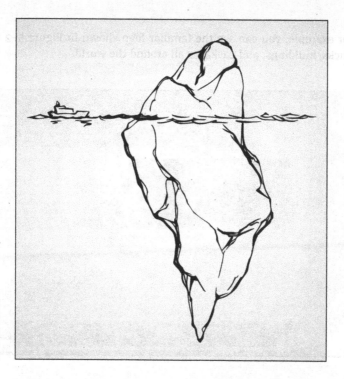

You can see a relationship between the items that appear above the waterline and those that appear below it. In most cases, the invisible aspects of culture influence or cause the visible ones. Religious beliefs, for example, may manifest in certain holiday customs, and notions of modesty can affect style of dress.

TIP

Behavior isn't spontaneous for the most part; the way people act and interact with others is based on their culture. The behavior of a person from another culture may be different from how you'd act in the same situation, and that's because the customs of your two cultures are different. People behave the way they do based on what they believe or value.

Celebrating Diversity

Genuinely understanding and accepting another culture can be difficult. Often, you may interpret what you see and hear through the lens of what you expect to see and hear, but that interpretation may not be accurate when you're interacting with people from another culture.

For example, you can see the familiar logo shown in Figure 5-2 on the sides of trucks, buildings, and packages all around the world.

FIGURE 5-2:
The FedEx logo.

The FedEx logo is easily recognizable. But have you really examined it? Take a closer look. Have you ever noticed the arrow hidden in the logo? It's right there between the E and the x.

The point I'm making here is that sometimes seeing something or someone a different way takes a little work, and that's why I encourage you to look at a different culture or a diverse group and see them as they truly are and not as you suspect or imagine they may be.

WARNING

If you're looking for what you want to see, or think you know exactly what you'll see, you may not notice the positive differences that are so important. You have to be open to the beauty of diversity that's right in front of you.

Understanding individuals' differences

Even when you know that celebrating diversity is important to your personal and professional success, you may sometimes struggle to accept the diversity you encounter and gravitate toward people who are most like you and provide a sense of familiarity. You may not even be aware that you're doing so, but you're not alone.

During childhood, people are conditioned by their experiences and environments to seek out what's the same and to avoid what's different. Each person is raised to view and to react to the world around them in certain ways, and these unique differences shape a person's appearance, language, and behavior. These differences — along with cultural beliefs, traditions, and religion — shape each person's current view of themselves, others, and the world, which is why learning to understand and accept other cultures can sometimes be difficult.

WARNING

Because you look at people from another culture through your "me" filter, you may need to work to learn how to see and accept something or someone in a different way.

Accepting that seeing is not always believing

You probably believe that you see things as they truly are. However, your mind interprets what your eyes see and gives those things meaning. In other words, what you see is as much in your mind as it is in reality.

When you consider that the mind of a person from one culture is going to assign different meaning to things than the mind of a person from another culture is, you've just arrived at the most fundamental of all cross-cultural problems: the fact that two people look at the same situation and see two entirely different things.

Any behavior observed across the cultural divide has to be interpreted two ways:

>> The meaning given to it by the person who performs the action

>> The meaning given to it by the person who observes the action

REMEMBER

Only when these two meanings are the same do you have successful cross-cultural communication. And by *successful*, I'm saying that the meaning the doer intended is the same as the meaning the observer understood.

Understanding interpretation is an important part of cultivating cultural awareness, so here's a quick exercise to make the concept a little easier to understand:

Read the following five behavior scenarios and write your immediate interpretation of that behavior in terms of your own cultural values, beliefs, or perceptions. Don't give your responses too much thought. Just write what immediately comes to mind.

1. A person comes to a meeting half an hour after the stated starting time. Your interpretation:

_____

_____

2. A person you're having a conversation with doesn't look you in the eyes when speaking to you. Your interpretation:

_____

_____

3. Two people are kissing each other while seated on a park bench. Your interpretation:

_____

_____

4. Someone gives you the thumbs-up gesture. Your interpretation:

_____

Your personal interpretation of each situation determined where your mind went as you were reading each of these situational sentences. For example, you may have read item 4 and thought that the person was giving you a sign of encouragement or approval. However, in some Middle Eastern countries, giving someone a thumbs-up gesture sends the same message as raising a different finger in the United States. (Yep. *That one.*)

REMEMBER

Personal interpretations aren't right or wrong. They're personal. Everyone has their own interpretation of any situation, and respecting the fact that their interpretation isn't right or wrong is important. After you understand and accept that interpretations are a personal matter, you can begin to cultivate tolerance and respect for others who see things differently than you do.

Saying No to Stereotyping

Fostering the ability to understand, embrace, and respect the differences you see in others is critical to your success in the workplace and in life. One of the first and most significant steps in the process is to admit that you have personal biases, prejudices, and the tendency to apply stereotypes to others.

REMEMBER

All people have some biases and prejudices. Biases, prejudices, and the tendency to stereotype are culturally divisive behaviors that many (or maybe even most) people are prone to. After you become culturally aware and work not to act on those biases and prejudices, you can make positive and permanent work and life changes.

Prejudice is being down on something you're not up on.

Stereotyping is the practice of assuming that similar people or groups of people think, act, look, feel, and believe the same things simply because they share the same culture. When you stereotype people, you prejudge them.

Stereotyping tends to dehumanize people by lumping them all together. And no one wants that. Every person wants to be seen for who they are as an individual. Feeling negative about a certain person or avoiding a certain group of people simply because they're different from you can minimize your worldview and affect your ability to work well with others.

You may believe that you always treat others you meet as equals, but this ideal probably isn't true at times, and you may not even realize you're violating it. According to stereotyping studies, most people have biases and prejudices they aren't even aware of that can have a major influence on the way they interact with others.

Stepping on the stereotyping scale

The first step to avoiding unconscious stereotyping behaviors is to identify the ways you may be practicing stereotyping. Grab your pen and paper and write your first thought that completes the following statements:

>> All famous movie and television stars . . .

_____

_____

>> All professional athletes . . .

_____

_____

>> All vegetarians . . .

_____

_____

>> All men with long hair . . .

_____

_____

>> All women with tattoos . . .

_____

_____

>> All politicians . . .

_____

_____

Take a look at your responses. Did they come easily to you? If so, you may have a tendency to stereotype the people you meet at work and in life. Were most of your responses positive or negative? If they were mostly negative, you may have a tendency to be prejudiced and biased when meeting someone new and different from you.

REMEMBER

Any sentence about people that begins with the word *all* is stereotypical from the start.

Recognizing how you stereotype

REMEMBER

Education is the key to change, and right here and now is a great opportunity to start educating yourself. After you begin to recognize your biases, prejudices, and tendency to stereotype, you can use your newly acquired knowledge to develop and practice a culture of tolerance, acceptance, and celebration both in the workplace and in life.

The power of daily active practice, practice, practice improves your diversity and cultural awareness skills and leads to career and life success. Employers want to hire and promote people who work well with others.

Use the following three simple exercises for daily practice in respecting diversity and developing cultural awareness:

>> **Become aware.** Take the time to acknowledge your cultural conditioning and identify your stereotypes, biases, and prejudices. Be brave enough to reflect on both the positive and negative aspects of your own diversity and examine why you think the way you do. This process has you question things that you may never have questioned before.

OPENING YOUR MIND

Wouldn't the world be a wonderful, easy, and fun place to live and work if you could simply change color like a chameleon each time you encountered a new and different culture? Of course, you can't change the way you look, but by cultivating cultural awareness and cross-cultural communication skills, you can change the way you think and how you communicate with people whose cultures differ from your own.

The more people know about the world's different cultures, the better able they are to understand and accept their differences. When people understand and accept one another, the world naturally becomes a wonderful, easy, and fun place to live and work!

>> **Educate yourself.** Make an effort to learn more about cultural practices from other countries — their etiquette, traditions, and acceptable forms of communication. Make a genuine effort with your culturally diverse co-workers to learn about and respect your differences and to find similarities you can build on.

>> **Show respect.** When you demonstrate the same respect to others that you want to receive from them, you're acknowledging that you value all people, not only those who look, think, talk, and act the way you do. Each person is a unique individual, and everyone has much to contribute.

TIP

Differences will always exist. Diversity will always be a part of the workplace and life. And that's a good thing! All you have to do to learn how to respect diversity and cultivate cultural awareness is to remember that your mind is like a parachute: It works best when it's open.

Looking at Real-Life Scenarios: The Newcomer

A new hire is in the office today, and the office manager has chosen two company employees to spend the day introducing their new co-worker to the other employees, giving a tour of the facility, and generally showing them the ropes.

>> **Getting it wrong:** The first employee chosen to welcome the new hire is thrilled to have been given this company honor; it shows that their manager

considers them a good employee example and a potential leader. This employee walks proudly into the front lobby, takes one look at the way the new hire is dressed, and smiles and shakes the new co-worker's hand. But in their mind, this employee is stereotyping up a storm: *They probably don't speak English. They probably eat strange food. They probably won't get along with the rest of us. They aren't the same as we are. Why do they dress like that? Don't they know it makes them stand out as weird and different? Why can't they dress like the rest of us at work? Why can't they just fit in? What a waste of time this day will be. Why did the boss have to choose me?*

» **Getting it right:** The second employee chosen to welcome the new hire is also thrilled to have been given this company honor; it shows that the manager considers them a warm and friendly person and a good company representative. This employee walks happily into the front lobby, takes one look at the way the new hire is dressed, smiles, and warmly shakes the new co-worker's hand. Their mind follows this train of thought: *How fun! Someone new and different. Something new to learn. Maybe a new friend. Someone to eat lunch with in the cafeteria. I can't wait to hear about their culture. This is going to be a great day! Not the same old, same old. How did I get so lucky?*

VOICES OF INDUSTRY

Karin Morrison

Chief Executive Officer

American Hospitality Academy

Karin has an extensive 20-plus-year background in the hospitality industry. She has been recognized for her leadership and contribution to service excellence and business development through her dedication and ability to inspire and motivate her team. Karin has been the Regional Director of Human Resources for various management companies and leading hotel chains of the world, including Marriott, Hilton, Hyatt, and Ritz-Carlton, as well as independent luxury resorts. Karin reflects on how soft skills play a role in the hospitality industry:

The American Hospitality Academy (AHA) connects young people from around the world with life-changing international cultural exchange opportunities. AHA helps future hospitality leaders become the best versions of themselves by developing the skills and attitude needed to make a difference in themselves and a difference in the world.

As the past Human Resources Director and now CEO at AHA, I have worked with countless hospitality industry professionals. When asked what skills they most often hire for, the answer is always "a hospitality attitude." A hospitality attitude is a passion for guest service and the soft skills needed to relate to and serve customers, communicate with fellow workers and customers, and ensure customers are satisfied with the service provided.

When you display the essential soft skills in the hospitality industry, you develop positive relationships between guests and your teammates. This allows you to have positive interpersonal communications with others and to implement your personal responsibilities to help fulfill guests' needs and meet company goals.

Soft skills such as cultural understanding, communication, time management, leadership, respect for others, attention to detail, problem solving, teamwork, flexibility, and work ethic are essential to a successful and happy career in the hospitality industry.

P.S.: They make life more fun, too!

Chapter **6**

Making an Impression with Your Appearance and Manners

S ome soft skills go hand in hand, and appearance and etiquette are such a pair. (Attitude, which I cover in Chapter 2, and character, which is the topic of Chapter 3, are another dynamic duo.) Appearance is the way you look. Etiquette is the way you act. These two soft skills work together to create that all-important first (and lasting) impression you make in both work and personal situations.

In this chapter, I explain the importance of making positive first impressions that lead to lasting success. I also introduce you to the elements of presenting a nice appearance and demonstrating good etiquette.

Acing the Four-Second First Impression

As the old adage says, you rarely get a second chance to make a good first impression. That means you need to try to get it right from the start.

Believe it or not, you have only four seconds to make a positive impression when you meet someone for the first time. Yep. Four seconds! That's barely enough time to say, "Hello, I'm Cindi. It's nice to meet you," much less do anything else.

That four-second impression may not seem fair, but it's a fact. Regardless of whether the people you meet would say so (and whether they're right), they think they have you totally figured out based on how you look when they first meet you. Your grooming habits and how they affect your appearance have a huge effect on what kind of person a new acquaintance thinks you are and what kind of future employee you may be.

For career and life success, your personal appearance (cleanliness, clothing, body language) matters — a lot. Your four-second first impression can make or break a job interview. A positive first impression can open doors, and a negative one can close them (and minds).

Here's an example. Take a four-second look at each of the photos shown in Figure 6-1. Make sure to count four seconds and then quickly decide who these people are based only on what you see. What are your first impressions of the people pictured? What does each person's expression say to you?

You don't know the people in Figure 6-1, but you've formed an immediate opinion about each of them based entirely on how they look this first time you're seeing them. See how fast first impressions — right or wrong — are formed?

FIGURE 6-1:
A person's facial expression influences a first impression.

Stepping on the Appearance and Etiquette Scale

What kind of first personal impression do you think you make on others? Are you neat as a pin or a little slapdash when you're getting dressed? Do you have a regular personal hygiene routine? Do you think good manners matter? To find out where you stand on the appearance and etiquette scale, read the following statements and choose the response for each that best describes you.

I keep my clothes clean and well pressed.		
Always	Sometimes	Never

I keep my hair clean and well groomed.		
Always	Sometimes	Never

I dress appropriately for work and social occasions.		
Always	Sometimes	Never

Personal hygiene is important to me.		
Always	Sometimes	Never

My appearance makes a good first impression.		
Always	Sometimes	Never

I make eye contact when communicating with others.		
Always	Sometimes	Never

When meeting someone new, I offer a handshake and a smile.		
Always	Sometimes	Never

People say I have good manners.		
Always	Sometimes	Never

I act appropriately at work and in social situations.		
Always	Sometimes	Never

I'm courteous and polite to everyone I meet.		
Always	Sometimes	Never

If you mostly responded to the statements with "always," you're likely making friends and influencing people like wildfire. If you most often responded "sometimes," you're halfway there. A little appearance and etiquette polishing should do the job. If you most often responded "never," you've got some work cut out for you cultivating the kind of appearance and etiquette skills that lead to career and life success.

Better keep yourself clean and bright; you are the window through which you must see the world.

—GEORGE BERNARD SHAW

Looking the Part: Why Appearance Matters

Making a positive first impression on others starts with your physical appearance, or what I like to call "looking the part." Looking the part helps you play the part, and after you've figured out how to play the part to perfection, it becomes a normal habit in your routine. Like everything in life, however, figuring out how to present yourself to make a positive first impression takes practice.

Putting your best foot (and face) forward

A true and genuine smile is one of the best and cheapest ways to improve your personal appearance. The most expensive designer outfit in the world isn't going to make much of a positive impression if you're wearing a scowl. When you smile, your appearance instantly says to the world, "I'm approachable. I'm agreeable. I'm open."

Smiling when you feel happy is easy, but when you feel upset or nervous, as you may when you're meeting someone new, you may need to put a little bit of effort into using your smile. Research shows that when you make yourself smile, even when you don't feel like smiling, you actually start to feel happier, and happy people make good first impressions. So practice your smile right now — even if you don't feel like it.

The energy you put into the way you walk and speak also influences how you feel. If you walk with a spring in your step and speak with energy in your voice, you'll feel energetic and springy, too. That's the meaning behind the saying "Fake it till you make it." Consciously putting effort into presenting a pleasant facial expression and posture can have a positive effect on what you feel subconsciously, too.

TIP

Smiling people are more approachable and seem more interesting than frowning people. A smiling person seems confident and tends to attract other smiling people. So when you get dressed each day, remember to put a smile on your face before you walk out the door.

A smile is the light in your window that tells others that there is a caring, sharing person inside.

—DENIS WAITLEY

Dressing for success

The way you dress affects the way you feel and act as well as the way others react to you. Like your smile, what you wear says a lot to the world about you.

Personal styles and preferences vary from person to person. Clothes can be an expression of individuality and creativity, and that's perfectly fine in certain situations — for example, when you're hanging out with your friends or attending a family gathering. I call this approach "dressing to express." In other circumstances, such as a job interview or an important meeting with someone, conforming to a certain standard of dress is more important for making a good first impression. I describe this manner of dressing as "dressing for success."

TIP

The best rule to follow in both workplace and social situations is to dress the way you want to be addressed. In other words, select the outfit you wear for an occasion based on how you want people to react when they see you. Think of your purpose, the place, the time of year, and even the time of day and choose clothes that help you look the part you want to portray.

WARNING

A dress code exists in the real world, and unfortunately people often are judged simply by their appearance. Making snap judgments about who someone is based on the way they're dressed may not be fair, but it happens every day, and you need to be prepared for it. No matter what you choose to wear for any given situation, making sure your clothes look fresh and clean is important. Keeping your clothes well pressed keeps you from looking hard pressed.

Acting the Part: Why Etiquette Is Important

People form a first impression largely based on how you look, but after you get past the initial four seconds, etiquette, or acting the part, comes in. (Flip to the earlier section "Acing the Four-Second First Impression" for more on this lightning-fast judgment.)

You can think of *etiquette* as your personal and professional code of conduct. It's the way you act in the workplace and out in the world. The personal and professional behaviors you choose to display every day determine how your employers, co-workers, family, and friends see you and how they choose to behave toward you in return.

REMEMBER

To state it very simply: *Manners matter.* It's nice to be important, but it's more important to be nice.

Exhibiting good personal and professional manners enables you to connect with your fellow employees, impress your employers, make friends, strengthen relationships, show respect, get respect, and build confidence in all workplace and life situations.

To make a pleasant and friendly impression is not alone good manners, but equally good business.

—EMILY POST

Shaking on it

A handshake is a first-impression gesture acknowledged around the world, and some handshakes make a better impression than others. With practice, you can develop a handshake that isn't too firm, too tight, or too loose. To make a good first impression, your handshake should be firm and positive but not overpowering. It should speak for you, communicating confidence, warmth, honesty, friendliness, and strength.

You cannot shake hands with a clenched fist.

—INDIRA GANDHI

Speaking volumes with manners

Some manners send a verbal message, and some speak physically. Use the following ten tips to help you cultivate good etiquette:

» Speak politely.

» Make eye contact during conversations.

» Shake hands when greeting someone. Refer to the preceding section for info on handshakes.

» Open and hold doors for others.

» Say "please" and "thank you."

» Address people respectfully in the manner of their choice by using their preferred pronouns and prefixes and (where appropriate) "sir" and "ma'am."

» Wait your turn.

» Be a good listener.

> » Greet others with a handshake and a smile.

> » Put your phone down at work and in social situations.

REMEMBER

Social customs vary from place to place, so when you're going to someplace that's new to you, take some time to learn about the customs so that you are prepared when you arrive.

Sharing your positive energy

When you focus your positive energy toward others, positive energy comes back to you. Here's an example: The next time you're on a crowded bus or subway, offer your seat to someone who's standing. Or let the person behind you in the grocery store line take your place. Stand back with a smile and say, "Go right ahead. After you." People are very appreciative of these types of kindnesses, and you may be surprised at the smile you get in return.

Walking your talk

When you *walk your talk*, you put your words into action. You do what you say you're going to do when you say you're going to do it. Lots of people are good at the talk, but far fewer are good at the walk. For example, if you don't intend to actually show up to work the company picnic dunking booth, don't sign up to do it. If you don't plan to put your whole heart into coaching a local sports team, don't volunteer for the position. Saying you'll do something when you know you probably won't is rude. It's bad manners. Worse, it leaves others having to pick up your slack, which is going to leave them with a negative impression of you.

Looking at Real-Life Scenarios: A Striking Difference

Two job applicants are finalists for the same high school teaching position. On paper, the applicants are equally qualified. They arrive for their personal interviews on exactly the same day at exactly the same time, and that's where their similarities end and their differences become apparent.

> » **Getting it wrong:** Teacher applicant one looks like one of the high school students they hope to be teaching. This person is wearing casual clothes — jeans, a wrinkled button-down rolled at the sleeves, and unlaced sneakers.

This applicant thinks they look the part. They know they're smart and capable, and the kids will like them. In this person's opinion, what they know is what counts; what they show doesn't matter.

When the superintendent calls this applicant in for their interview, they pull out their earbuds and slide their phone into their back pocket. They give the superintendent a grin and a head nod as they say, "Hey. What's up?"

>> **Getting it right:** Teacher applicant two seems to have taken great care with their appearance. Their clothes are classroom appropriate, clean, and neatly pressed, and they've paid attention to their hair and personal hygiene. When this applicant introduces themself to the school superintendent, they make eye contact; give a warm, bright smile; and offer a firm and confident hand-shake as they say, "Thank you for taking the time to meet with me today. I'm excited about this position and the benefits I believe I can bring to your school and your students."

So finish the story. Which applicant do you think got the position, and which applicant is still looking for a job?

When you look and act the part, it's easier to get — and keep — the part.

VOICES OF INDUSTRY

Faye Washington

President and CEO

YWCA Greater Los Angeles

Established in 1894, the YWCA Greater Los Angeles's mission is to eliminate racism, empower women, and promote peace, justice, freedom, and dignity for all. It operates housing, seven Empowerment Centers, and five satellite offices in low-income, histori-cally underserved communities in Downtown, East, and South Los Angeles as well as in the South Bay. The signature programs under its Equity Model include Child Development (childcare and resources); Workforce Development; and Senior, Youth, and Sexual Assault Crisis Services. For decades, the YWCA Greater Los Angeles has put satisfying careers within reach of disconnected youth and adults with high barriers to employment.

Based on my 32 years in government and 22 years as the YWCA GLA's President and CEO, I am convinced that soft skills such as interpersonal communication, critical thinking,

(continued)

(continued)

leadership, and resilience are the cornerstone of success in the workplace and providing access to opportunity. I believe people skills are a unique common denominator that is the advancement for generations to come. Through the years, I have witnessed our community youth who have struggled to succeed, who encounter so many barriers to a secure and stable future. In providing access to opportunity, we must do more than open a few doors. We strive to expose our participants to realities they never dreamed were possible and equip them with marketable, sought-after soft skills through high-quality training, sharing both confidence and belief in their tomorrow — this is true access.

It is proven that providing soft skills coupled with workforce innovation provides access to a high-quality career and technical education, resulting in industry-certified graduates who then can be placed in sustainable career paths. I have always recognized that the "playing field" will never truly be level for the disadvantaged; however, we work to create access and opportunity for our participants that will benefit them and generations to come.

Chapter **7**

Staying on Top of Things with Time Management

You have 24 hours in each day. Not one more. Not one less. Money can't buy you more time, and you can't save time for a rainy day. You either use it or you lose it.

Successful people choose to use their time wisely. They make the most of their daily allotment of time both at work and in life. They understand that taking charge of their time puts them in charge of their lives.

In this chapter, I explain the importance of cultivating good time management skills and offer ways to use those skills to effectively take control of your life in a positive and productive way.

Don't count every hour in the day. Make every hour in the day count.

—ALFRED BINET

Stepping on the Time Management Scale

A wise — and successful — person once said, "You can manage your money, or it can manage you." The same is true with your time. A person who manages their time well is dependable, accountable, responsible, reliable, and punctual. Often, people who have good time management are also successful, largely because they get where they need to be on time. People who don't manage their time well are often late to the party, so to speak, and they miss out on opportunities for career and life success.

REMEMBER

To be functional, you must be punctual.

One way that managing time is no different from any other soft skill is that how you choose to spend your time is 100 percent up to you. You can take control of it, or you can let it manage you.

You can do a simple assessment to see how well you use your time. For the following statements, a score of 1 means "not like me at all" and 5 means "very much like me." Record your score for each question to see where you fall on the time management scale. Be honest with your scoring.

TAKING IT TO THE BANK

Imagine a bank credits your account each morning with $1,440. At the end of the day, no remaining balance carries to the next day. In other words, every evening, whatever money you didn't use during the day just disappears. What would you do? Draw out every cent, of course!

You may not have this sort of bank that holds money, but you do have such a bank of time.

Every morning, your time bank credits you with 1,440 minutes. Every night it writes off as lost whatever time you haven't invested to good purpose. No balance carries over to the next day. You're not allowed an overdraft. A new account opens for you each day. If you don't use the day's deposits, the loss is yours, and you can't draw against tomorrow. You must live in the present on today's time deposit. Spend your time wisely so you get the most you can from it in health, happiness, and success.

I hardly ever make a commitment for a deadline I can't keep.				
1	2	3	4	5

I generally answer emails and return phone calls right away.				
1	2	3	4	5

After I have the information I need, I usually make decisions quickly.				
1	2	3	4	5

I'm able to fit an unscheduled action item into my day.				
1	2	3	4	5

I feel satisfied with what I've accomplished at the end of the week.				
1	2	3	4	5

I seldom find myself running out of time.				
1	2	3	4	5

I generally like to focus on one thing at a time.				
1	2	3	4	5

I rarely procrastinate.				
1	2	3	4	5

I often don't get jobs done for days, even if they require little effort to sit down and do them.				
1	2	3	4	5

I frequently leave things for tomorrow.				
1	2	3	4	5

When faced with a huge task, I break it into chunks and figure out what to do first so I can get going.				
1	2	3	4	5

I often have a task finished sooner than necessary.				
1	2	3	4	5

I never waste time looking for things. I know where everything is.				
1	2	3	4	5

When deadlines get close, I often waste time doing other things.				
1	2	3	4	5
I find saying no to requests that aren't in my priorities easy.				
1	2	3	4	5

Scoring:

>> 44–50 points: This score is excellent! Your time management skills are sharp.

>> 31–45 points: This rating is very good, but you can make better use of your time.

>> 15–30 points: The good news is you've got all the time in the world to improve this score. I discuss ways you can achieve better time management in the following sections.

Taking Back Control of Your Time

When you don't have control of your time management, you're often late, behind at work, unproductive, unreliable, and most likely stressed. When your timing is off, you're often "off" as well.

If you regularly think *That can wait until tomorrow* or *I'll save that for the weekend when I have more time*, know that your tomorrow is probably overbooked, too. To successfully manage your time at work and in life, you have to understand that what you accomplish today determines the brightness of tomorrow's future. That's where good time management skills come in. Bonus: When you choose to become the manager of your minutes, you discover what it means to have time on your side.

Trading being busy for being productive

There's a big difference between being busy and being productive. Busy people may seem productive because they always have so much to do. But in reality, most busy people have fallen behind and are constantly racing against the clock to catch up or keep up. Good time management isn't measured by how much you have to do in a day. It's about what you actually get done in a day — what you get accomplished.

Three things you can do immediately to start taking better control of your time are

>> Scheduling your time

>> Being accountable

>> Taking initiative

Scheduling your time

Scheduling is a huge component of successful time management and being productive. Creating a schedule that reflects your work priorities and responsibilities while also supporting your personal goals is a winning combination. *Remember:* Along with scheduling priority tasks, you also need to make time for those inevitable interruptions and unexpected events that can knock your time management train off the track.

Keeping a daily schedule is one of the best tools to manage your time. When you write your schedule for your day or keep track of it in a calendar app, you are able to plan your day's activities, which allow you to use your time efficiently and hit your goals. When you schedule your day you

>> Set goals that are achievable

>> Stay focused to help avoid interruptions

>> Help balance your life between work, social, and family obligations

To schedule a day that is productive, keep the following:

>> **Know what your desired outcome is.** In other words, what do you want to have achieved by the end of the day?

>> **Select a scheduling method and stick with it.** Find the planner, app, or digital calendar that works best for you and use it daily.

>> **Create a routine each day.** Find a reason that motivates you to get your day started and tackle what is on your schedule.

>> **Organize and prioritize your tasks.** Sometimes doing the harder things first is a better reward. Regardless of whether you tackle the hard things first or save them for later, be organized in your approach to what you need to accomplish.

>> **Schedule unexpected events.** Technically, you can't schedule unexpected events or tasks, but you can schedule some free time, which gives you an opportunity to take care of unplanned interruptions.

Being accountable

Accountability means taking responsibility for the way you choose to spend your time. If you show up late for work because you chose to hit the snooze button one too many times, you're responsible for that mistake — not someone else. It's also not someone else's fault if you can't find the time to return phone calls and emails.

REMEMBER

Being accountable means that you take responsibility both for how you choose to use your time and for the results of the choices you make, positive and negative.

Taking initiative

People with good time management skills take initiative and take action. Think back to a time in your childhood when you were consumed with wanting to learn how to do something — for example, riding a bicycle, playing a video game, dancing, or playing the piano. You may have practiced this new skill hour after hour after hour and spent every free minute of your time determined to become proficient at it. You may have even sacrificed other things to make your dream come true. If you put a lot of time into your practice, you were probably very disciplined.

Are you bringing that focus, self-discipline, and passion for success to your career and life today? If not, why not, and what can you do to get it back?

TIP

To re-spark the passion and self-discipline you need to succeed at your job and in life, you have to constantly look for inspiration both within and without. You have to take initiative to find the motivation to excel at what you do. Without initiative on your part, procrastination sets in, and missed opportunities become every day occurrences. Following are some techniques that may help you maintain your motivation:

>> Break your work down into smaller steps that you cross off as you complete them.

>> Change your environment mid-day by taking the work outside for a little bit or sitting in a different area of the office.

>> Create a playlist that energizes you to finish your tasks.

>> Stay off of social media.

>> Give yourself a deadline for completing a task and try to meet (or beat) it.

>> Reward yourself after you finish a task. Get up, stretch, and pat yourself on the back.

Don't just dream and talk about doing something someday. Go out and do it, starting today, because you want to succeed tomorrow.

Giving up the excuses

When you start making good time management decisions and choices, you stop making excuses. Some people go through life as chronic underachievers because they blame anyone and anything other than themselves for their lack of time management skills. Chronic underachievers have two favorite statements:

>> **"It's not my fault."** No matter what the scenario is, when something goes wrong, they can come up with a million creative excuses to back up this statement. In fact, in a weird twist, underachievers actually become over-achievers when the task is "making excuses for not having enough time in a day to get things done."

>> **"Oops, I forgot!"** Being forgetful isn't a crime. It happens to people all the time. However, people with good time management skills don't lean on this phrase as an excuse. They know many tools are available to avoid the forgetfulness pitfall: sticky notes, phone alerts, day planners, and so on.

Becoming the manager of your minutes

The bad news is time flies. The good news is you're the pilot.
—MICHAEL ALTSHULER

Being the manager of your minutes is all about making your time work for you. To cultivate good time management skills, you need to be proactive about managing your responsibilities by setting priorities, creating a daily schedule and sticking to it.

The first order of business is to do the things that are absolutely necessary. When those tasks are done, you do the things that are possible. Lastly, you can do the things you want to do because you've made time for you. With a bit of priority practice, you become less busy and more productive, so you can start ticking items off your once impossibly long list left and right. (I cover the difference between busyness and productivity in "Trading being busy for being productive" earlier in the chapter.)

No matter where you currently stand on the time management scale, the follow-ing five-step process can help make the most of every day on your way up the ladder of career and life success. If you're unsure where your current time management skills fall on the spectrum, check out the assessment in the earlier section "Stepping on the Time Management Scale."

1. Make a commitment.

Make a conscious commitment to yourself to improve your organizational skills by planning and prioritizing. Put this promise at the top of your list each day. Tell yourself that you deserve to be the manager of your minutes. You deserve to have enough time each day to do what you need to do with enough time left over to do what you want to do.

2. Set goals.

For your daily commitment to pay off, you have to set reasonable and reachable goals for your 24-hour allotment of time each day. Start by setting daily goals. After you're regularly achieving the daily goals, you can move on to setting weekly and monthly goals. Before long, you can think even longer term and plan for career goals and retirement. It's all possible with good time management skills.

3. Get organized.

If you haven't discovered the satisfaction of crossing something off your to-do list, it's time you try it. First thing in the morning, take the time to make a list specifying the tasks you need to complete that day. Make it an achievable list, or you won't even want to get started. Check each task off your daily list as soon as you complete it. Uncapping that pen is surprisingly fun!

REMEMBER

If you're not at the end of your list at the end of the day, don't despair: You may have overcommitted. That's okay. Figuring out how many to-do items you can reasonably accomplish in a day takes practice. As you figure out how to manage your minutes better, you have more and more success getting to the end of your list each day.

4. Arrive on time.

What type of morning person are you? Do you repeatedly press the snooze button on your alarm, or do you promptly get out of bed on time? Do you show up for work each day fully awake and present? Are you 100 percent punctual and 100 percent functional?

People with good time management skills don't make a point to get wherever they're going (work, a family function) on time; they make a point to get there a few minutes early. They set the alarm fifteen minutes earlier than necessary each night. They give themselves the time they need to succeed.

AN EMPTY PICKLE JAR

A philosophy professor started a class by wordlessly picking up a very large, empty pickle jar and filling it with golf balls. They then asked the students if the jar was full. The students agreed that it was. Then the professor poured a box of pebbles into the jar and shook it lightly. The pebbles rolled into the open areas between the golf balls. The professor asked the students again if the jar was full, and the class again agreed it was.

The professor poured a box of sand into the jar. Of course, the sand filled in the even smaller cracks. They asked once more if the jar was full. The students responded with a unanimous "Yes." Finally, the professor produced two glasses of chocolate milk from under the table and poured the entire contents into the jar, effectively filling the empty space between the sand. The students laughed.

"Now," the professor said, "I want you to recognize that this jar represents your life. The golf balls are the important things: your family, your children, your health, your friends, your favorite passions. Things that if everything else was lost and only they remained, your life would still be full. The pebbles are the other things that matter like your job, your home, your car. The sand is everything else — the small stuff.

"If you put the sand into the jar first, you have no room for the pebbles or the golf balls. The same goes for life. If you spend all your time and energy on the small stuff, you'll never have room for the things that are critical to your happiness.

"Play with your children. Take time to get medical checkups. Take your partner to dinner. Play another 18 holes. You'll always find time to clean the house or fix the disposal. Take care of the golf balls — the things that really matter — first. Set your priorities. The rest is just sand."

A student said, "But what about the chocolate milk?"

The professor smiled and said, "No matter how full your life may seem, there will always be room for chocolate."

REMEMBER

Being chronically late, even by just a few minutes, isn't an inherited condition. It's a learned behavior pattern. It's also rude and disrespectful behavior, and it often leads to lack of professional success. Fortunately, you can unlearn the behavior.

5. Take time for you.

Penciling in a little personal time for yourself each day is important. If you don't plan some time for yourself to do what you want to do, chances are you'll feel cheated from the outset and choose to let something on your daily to-do list go undone. Any small break in the day can help refresh you and make you more prepared to get back to your task list: a morning yoga class, a brisk walk at lunch, a short conversation with a co-worker about the previous night's game, an iced coffee in the afternoon, and so on. Think of it as a little personal reward for a daily time management job done well done.

You'll be surprised at how these little daily rewards increase both your productivity and your commitment to making the most of your time each day.

Looking at Real-Life Scenarios: Slow and Steady Wins the Race

Two first-year college roommates have the same weekly class schedule and are carrying the exact same number of semester credit hours. Like the rabbit in the fairy tale "The Tortoise and the Hare," roommate one gets the semester off to a lightning-quick start. In no time, they're one of the most popular people in the dorm, and they're cruising toward a perfect first semester grade point average. Roommate two is a bit slower off the college starting block.

>> **Getting it wrong:** Roommate one hits the campus grounds running, racing to and from every class, turning in weekly assignments two or three days early, signing up for extra credit projects, and joining every social club that attracts their attention. This student is busy, busy, busy, and soon both their school and social life are fully booked — totally overbooked, actually. By the midsemester break, roommate one can no longer keep up with the college pace. They turn in assignments late, their grades begin to slip, and they start to miss early morning classes trying to catch up on missed sleep. This student's life has become totally unmanageable. There just never seems to be enough time.

>> **Getting it right:** Roommate two is more of the slow-and-steady type. They know how to balance work and fun, and they make lists and set priorities and goals. Classes and grades come first. Social activities come second. This student makes a to-do list each week, and they follow it to the letter, crossing off each completed task with a sense of accomplishment. They don't try do too much but also don't do too little. Roommate two manages their time well and enjoys rewards of little daily treats and breaks that keep them refreshed and moving steadily forward. At the midsemester break, slow-and-steady roommate two is right on schedule. Their grades are good, their class attendance and assignments are impeccable, and they're having the time of their life.

So which roommate is likely to win the first-year race? Roommate two, who's in a much better position to actually cross the finish line despite roommate one's early lead.

VOICES OF INDUSTRY

Paul Pineiro, EdD

New Jersey Assistant Superintendent of Schools

With an educational career spanning 30 years and extensive experience at the high school level, Paul is passionate about the importance of teaching soft skills to students at early ages in schools. He wrote his dissertation on the topic of *noncognitive skills* (also known as soft skills) and the need for a standard policy for integrating these skills into school curriculums.

Without soft skills, hard skills do not work nearly as effectively. To illustrate this point and the impact soft skills have had on my life, I'd like to share what I call the "Gerry Lesson."

As a sophomore in high school, I kept the bench warm on my high school varsity basketball team. I worked hard in practice to help the starting players continually improve, and in my senior year the team won the New Jersey state championship. But this story is not about me. It's about Gerry.

Gerry was another hard-working bench player on another strong Jersey City team. One summer, we were both attending a basketball camp run by St. Anthony's High School icon Bob Hurley Sr. Coach Hurley was a nationally renowned figure who was as inspiring as he was intimidating. Gerry and I played on the B-level squad, while the elite high school players made up the A-level. Gerry worked as hard in the fourth quarter as he did in the first. On offense, he scored when he had the opportunity, but he was also quick to pass the ball to others who were in better position to score. He was a team player.

One day as Gerry and I settled down in the bleachers to watch the A-squad warm up, Coach Hurley came over and drew Gerry from the crowd and had him walk to the center of the court with him. As Gerry stood awkwardly next to him at center court, the coach began: "Gentlemen, this is Gerry. Gerry is a fine basketball player. And while he may not quite reach the level of talent that the A-squad players have, he does have an A-squad-level heart." Gerry shifted his weight back and forth. Coach chuckled. "And so . . . I'm going to have Gerry play on the A-level all-star squad tonight so that, hopefully, some of his heart, grit, attitude, and teamwork will rub off on you all."

Coach Hurley saw in Gerry what many people miss. A person can have the greatest concrete skills in any given field, but they need soft skills to take those talents to the next level. Skills such as perseverance, attitude, and the ability to connect with others in a spirit of teamwork determine the difference between being good and being great, getting hired or passed over, and being promoted in the workplace rather than stagnating.

The "Gerry Lesson" taught me at a young age that soft skills really do make the hard skills work.

IN THIS CHAPTER

» **Understanding the importance of teamwork**

» **Identifying the skills needed to develop effective teams**

» **Handling conflict in teams**

Chapter **8**

Navigating the Dynamics of Working with Others

The ability to work as part of a team is one of the most important skills you can have. People who are able to contribute their own ideas while working with others to create and develop projects and accomplish goals are happy, productive, and successful. In short, people learn and grow best as professionals when they have opportunities to work with other people. As the saying goes, teamwork makes the dream work!

In this chapter, I cover why being able to work as part of a team is so important. I also discuss what elements contribute to a good team and how to manage conflicts among team members.

No one can whistle a symphony. It takes an orchestra to play it.

—HALFORD E. LUCCOCK

Recognizing that Working as a Team Takes Work

Being independent and receiving praise for a job you've done well is great, but life isn't a solo act. In fact, it's absolutely teeming with teams: work teams, student project teams, sports teams, medical teams, parent-teacher organizations — the list goes on and on. So although having a sense of individuality is important, cultivating a strong set of teamwork skills is equally important for success.

Each member of a team has a specific role to play. Think about a professional football team. In some cases, only one player may be dancing in the end zone after a touchdown, but a team effort is what got the ball to the goal line. That's why the entire team celebrates when those six points go up on the board. Every single player on the team, both those on the field and those on the sideline, knows they've contributed to this successful end zone effort.

The teamwork concept also applies to the workplace and life. A single member of a team can't succeed without the help and support of all the teammates, no matter the team or how talented that one member may be. Sure, some people try to go it alone. You know the type. In sports, these "it's all about me" team members are called *ball hogs*. They never pass the ball or share the glory. They're only out for number one. In their opinion, they're the only star that needs to shine, and they'll tackle anyone who gets in their way. The problem with that attitude is that their teams rarely win.

TEAMWORK AND EGO: A FABLE

A frog asked two geese to take it south with them. At first, they resisted; they didn't see how it could be done. Finally, the frog suggested that the two geese hold a stick in their beaks, and then the frog would hold on to the stick with its mouth.

So off the unlikely threesome went, flying southward over the countryside. It was really quite a sight to see. People looked up and expressed great admiration at this demonstration of creative teamwork.

Someone said, "It's wonderful! Who was so clever to discover such a fine way to travel?" At which point the frog opened its mouth and said, "It was I," as it plummeted to the earth.

Stepping on the teamwork scale

Teamwork involves building relationships and working with other people by using the following important skills and habits:

>> Cooperation

>> Brainstorming

>> Interpersonal communication

>> Responsibility for doing your part

>> Respect for different opinions, ideas, customs, and individual preferences

When you take all five of these team building blocks and put them to work as a positive and productive team member, your chances for personal and professional success skyrocket.

Think about the last time you were in a team environment — regardless of whether you were at work or school or in a social setting — and had to work with others toward a common goal. How did you perform as part of the team? Were you a committed, cooperative, responsible, and respectful team member who was determined to contribute to the success of the overall team goal?

TIP

Part of being a successful team member is knowing what your personal strengths are and how to use them. The other part is recognizing when you need to ask for help and taking initiative to get that help.

Ten personal characteristics make up a positive and productive team member:

>> Reliability

>> Effective communication

>> Active listening

>> Participation

>> Willingness to share

>> Cooperation

>> Flexibility

>> Commitment

>> Problem solving

>> Respect

Choose your level of confidence in each of these characteristics in the following survey. Be honest! You're here to figure out how to succeed as a team member at work and in life. You need to know where you stand with these characteristics so you can cultivate them and continue your pursuit of being the best team member possible.

Reliability: You can be counted on to get the job done.		
Not so confident	Sort of confident	Really confident
Effective communication: You express your thoughts and ideas clearly and directly with respect for others.		
Not so confident	Sort of confident	Really confident
Active listening: You listen to and respect different points of view. Others can offer you constructive feedback without upsetting you or making you defensive.		
Not so confident	Sort of confident	Really confident
Participation: You're prepared and get involved in team activities.		
Not so confident	Sort of confident	Really confident
Willingness to share: You're willing to share information, experience, and knowledge with the group.		
Not so confident	Sort of confident	Really confident
Cooperation: You work with other members of the team to accomplish the job — no matter what.		
Not so confident	Sort of confident	Really confident
Flexibility: You adapt easily when the team changes direction or you're asked to try something new.		
Not so confident	Sort of confident	Really confident
Commitment: You're responsible and dedicated. You always give your best effort.		
Not so confident	Sort of confident	Really confident
Problem solving: You focus on solutions. You don't go out of your way to find fault in others.		
Not so confident	Sort of confident	Really confident
Respect: You always treat other team members with courtesy and consideration.		
Not so confident	Sort of confident	Really confident

If your rating responses are mostly "not so confident," you're still developing as a team player. You may want to ask a mentor or a confident team player colleague whom you trust to be both honest and kind to help you develop a plan for raising your teamwork confidence level. Don't be afraid to ask for help. It's what a productive team player does!

If your rating responses are mostly "sort of confident," you're pretty confident in your teamwork skills but you may need a little extra support or development in a few areas. Invite your mentor, a colleague, or a supervisor you know and trust to help you work on the characteristics you want to improve. Becoming a good team member takes time, energy, and dedication.

If your responses are mostly "really confident," you're truly confident in your talent as a successful team player. That's great! However, even the best team player can look for opportunities to sharpen their teamworking tools. Always strive to make improvements where you can.

Building a Strong Team

Putting together a strong team is about more than telling a group of random people to work together to achieve a goal. In this section, I share the concepts of team formation and cooperation.

Here's an exercise: Imagine you're stranded on a deserted island. You're allowed to choose five people to join your survival team and help you devise a plan for getting off the island. The teammates you choose can be entertainers, politicians, business people, friends, or family and can be alive or dead. Your choice of survival teammates is 100 percent up to you.

After you've selected your team, consider the following questions:

>> Are all five of your teammates in the same profession?

>> Do they all have the same ethnicity or cultural background?

>> Are they all the same age?

>> Do they all have the same personality? The same hobbies? The same level of education?

Strong, successful teams consist of members with a diversity of strengths, talents, ages, genders, and ethnicities. Think of it this way: If your list consisted of five of the world's best architects, your team could probably build a wonderful shelter and maybe even a boat, but what would you do for food and water? How would your team survive while you were building the shelter and boat?

The most successful teams are made up of many different types of people, with each team member playing a different but important role. So if you chose five different types of people for your imaginary team, congratulations! The chances of your team finding a way off the island are very good.

TIP

Diversity of perspectives and skills is a great benefit to any team, and the key to making a diverse group or team successful is to understand the people you're working with. In work and life opportunities, you may not always get to choose who's on your team, but you can still do your part to capitalize on the diversities of your teammates by listening and asking questions that draw out different viewpoints and ideas.

REMEMBER

Together everyone accomplishes more

Getting Your Team in Shape

Researchers believe five basic personality types exist, and each type tends to prefer a different shape: square, rectangle, triangle, circle, or squiggle. Knowing which shapes you and your fellow team members gravitate to can help you be a better and more productive person and team member. Take a look at the five shapes in Figure 8-1 and decide which shape you're most drawn to. No answer is more right than any other, so make sure to select the one that speaks to you most.

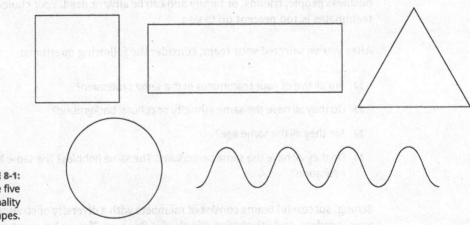

FIGURE 8-1:
The five
personality
shapes.

The following list describes the different traits attributed to the shapes according to the shape theory.

- » **Square:** Selecting the square shape indicates you're an organized, logical, and hardworking person who likes structure and rules. You can have trouble making decisions, however, because you always want more information. You feel most comfortable in a stable environment with clear directions on what to do. You tend to like things to be regular and orderly. You work on a task until it's finished, no matter what.

  Square personality types appear to move in a "straight" manner. They use precise and specific gestures, love routine, and are very focused on detail. Squares are very neat and organized in appearance and in their work area. They do a lot of planning and are always prompt.

- » **Rectangle:** Choosing the rectangle signals that you're a courageous, exciting, and inquisitive explorer who always searches for ways to grow and change. You enjoy trying things you've never done before and love asking questions that have never been asked. You like structure and are often the person to insist that things are done the proper way, taking all of the rules and regulations into consideration. When you get a task, you start organizing it to be sure you can do it in the most systematic way.

  Rectangle personality types often are described as having "fleeting eyes and flushed faces." They tend to giggle and like variety. They come into work early or stay late, but they usually aren't on time. Their personal workspaces tend to be somewhat disorganized.

- » **Triangle:** Picking the triangle shape to represent you is a sign that you're a born leader who is competitive and confident and can make decisions. You also like recognition. You're goal-oriented and enjoy planning well and then doing well. You're motivated by accomplishment. You tend to look at big, long-term issues, but you may overlook the small details. When you receive a task, you immediately set a goal and work on a plan to complete it. Many of the most successful U.S. companies have been run by triangles.

  Triangle personality types have powerful voices, love to tell jokes, and play as hard as they work.

- » **Circle:** Selecting the circle shape indicates that you're social and communicative. You have no hard edges. You handle things by talking about them and smoothing things out with everybody. Communication is your first priority. When you get a task, you want to talk about it. You're a people person with lots of sympathy and consideration for others. You listen and communicate well and are very perceptive about the feelings of others. You like harmony and hate making unpopular decisions.

Circle personality types are friendly, nurturing, persuasive, and generous. They tend to be relaxed and smile a lot. They're talkative but usually speak in a soft voice. They also have a full laugh and like to touch others on the shoulder or the arm when communicating.

>> **Squiggle:** Choosing the squiggle shape reflects that you're creative and like to think out of the box. You like doing new and different things and get bored with regularity. When you receive a task, you come up with bright and creative ideas about how to complete it, but you don't think in a deliberate pattern from point A to B to C. Instead, squiggles tend to jump around when approaching a task, going from point A to M to X.

Squiggle personality types are flashy, dramatic, and extremely creative, and they don't like highly structured environments. Squiggles tend to be funny and very expressive. They also have great intuition.

TIP

Each personality shape has strengths and weaknesses, so the best and most successful teams are made up of a combination of all five shapes.

Managing Team Conflict with Cooperation

Finding ways to work with a team of diverse personalities and talents helps you build relationships within a team. A diverse team allows its members to showcase their individual strengths, making determining which team role best suits each team member easier. No matter which personality type a person is, they have individual talents and skills that can help others succeed. And others, in turn, have something to offer that person.

This is where cooperation and conflict management come into play.

As I note earlier in the chapter, cooperation is one of the most important qualities of a great team player and future leader. If you can get along and cooperate with others in a team environment, you're setting yourself up for a great future.

When people who are working together cooperate, projects and communication run smoothly. Cooperative people do the following things:

>> Make each team member feel heard and respected

>> Listen to other team members

>> Give others positive feedback

>> Ask questions and request clarification when they're not sure about something

>> Contribute their thoughts and experience when discussing items with the team

Successful team members have also mastered the art of conflict management, which is one of the most challenging soft skills to cultivate. When team members can efficiently and effectively work together to create cooperative solutions to manage conflict, they're able to keep the group focused on the ultimate goal.

When team conflict arises, a solution always exists, though seeing it may be hard in the moment. When a situation heats up and you're trying your best to cool things down, having a conflict management plan on hand can help your team come together in a spirit of cooperation to find a workable solution. The following four-step conflict solution plan is one option:

1. Identify the conflict.

You can't solve a conflict if you don't know what the problem is. Identify the conflict and try to use it as an opportunity to strengthen the team.

2. Share and listen.

Allow each team member to share their perception of and feelings about the conflict and listen to the ideas of the group.

3. Brainstorm.

Work as a team to brainstorm solution ideas, using the information gathered from sharing and listening in Step 2.

4. High five.

After you've reached a solution and agreed on it peacefully and positively, celebrate as a reunited team and move on toward the shared goal.

I have learned how to hold a team together. How to lift some men up, how to calm down others, until finally they've got one heartbeat together, a team. There are three things I always say: If anything goes bad, I did it. If anything goes semi-good, then we did it. If anything goes real good, then you did it.

—BEAR BRYANT

Looking at Real-Life Scenarios: Picking a Dream Team

Two top-level managers have been given the task of selecting a five-member dream team to work on an important company project. They each have the same pool of 20 employees to choose from, and they each know the pool of employees well. That's where the similarities in this corporate team building story end.

» **Getting it wrong:** Top-level manager one makes their five top picks without hesitation. The dream team is made up of people the manager likes, people who will agree with whatever the manager says, and people who won't speak up. This manager knows best how the project should get done, and they don't want to have to deal with any conflict of interest or differing opinions among the team members. The manager is going to be the star of the project show, so they pick five team members that they know will stand back and let the manager shine.

» **Getting it right:** Top-level manager two goes about picking their dream team quite a bit differently. They're a square personality type (see the "Getting Your Team in Shape" section earlier in this chapter), and they know it. They understand their strengths and weaknesses and know they need to build a team that will be the best for the project, not for their ego. The manager goes through the employee pool list slowly and carefully. They choose each team member for their personality strengths and weaknesses. The manager doesn't choose their friends or people who will agree with whatever they say. They choose a rectangle, a circle, a triangle, and two squiggles (because they know squiggles are creative and creativity is essential to the success of this project).

VOICES OF INDUSTRY

Marcia Dmochowski

Retired General Manager

Hilton

Marcia is a graduate of Cornell School of Hotel Administration. She has more than 43 years in the hospitality industry and was the third female general manager for Hilton Hotels. Besides working for Hilton Hotels, Marcia worked for Marriott, Hyatt, Westin, and Sheraton.

There is a saying here at Hilton that says, "Find work that works for you — find your thing!"

When people find a job with Hilton, they are instantly welcomed in the family. Hilton helps you find your "thing"! Its thing is hospitality. It offers each applicant the freedom and flexibility of finding that one thing that they can turn into an exciting and fulfilling career.

As of 2022, the hospitality industry accounts for 10 percent of the overall employment in the United States. That translates to 8 million jobs, and the sector is expected to add another 3.3 million jobs by 2032. Hospitality and tourism lead the future as one of the largest growing work segments, offering career-minded young people a rewarding, fast-paced environment with multiple career paths.

Hilton's commitment to inspiring people so they can be their best encompasses guests, colleagues, and the community. When looking for new employees, we look for people who have the hospitality spirit, motivation to work hard, and desire to learn and grow within the company. We notice those with soft skills are already one step closer to being part of the Hilton family.

In the hospitality industry, soft skills are critical for success. For leaders as well as associates, these skills are what our industry is built upon. The ability to communicate on all levels is so important. Being able to "read" your audience and deliver the message in a way that it will be received positively to generate the desired result is a great asset to have not only for leaders but also for associates as the associates are dealing with the guests and many times can't deliver on their requests. How this information is given to the guests often determines if a manager then needs to get involved.

The ability to work as a team is a vital part of success. This often involves consideration of others, listening, contributing, and participating. In this new post-COVID-19 environment, we're all operating with less, which makes teamwork imperative for success.

Chapter 9

Applying Critical Thinking to Problems

Why is the moon round? Why is the sky blue? Why did the flower die? Why is the stove hot? *Why* are children always asking why, why, why? The answer is easy: because curiosity helps people learn about the world around them.

Asking questions is the brain's way of attempting to create order and understand the things you see and experience. As people age, their childlike wonder and tendency to question what they see and experience often falls by the wayside.

To some degree, this decline in curiosity may happen because people stop thinking for themselves. They become accustomed to being told what to think by society and cultural customs. The more a person is told *what*, the less they question *why*.

In this chapter, I explore the concept of critical thinking and explain why cultivating this soft skill is critical to career and life success.

Defining Critical Thinking

Critical thinking is self-directed, self-disciplined, self-monitored, and self-corrective thinking. It's the ability to absorb important information and use that information to form your own opinions and make your own decisions in life and at work.

Critical thinking is also the ability to make personal judgments that are logical and well thought out. It's a way of thinking that involves cultivating a genuinely curious attitude. It requires that you have your own point of view instead of simply parroting the people around you.

Every day, you have the opportunity to use the process of critical thinking to make decisions, solve problems, and communicate effectively. Critical thinking applies to all areas of life, whether it's picking out an outfit for the day, getting to school or work on time, or creating a five-year plan for your future.

Avoiding the lazy thinking rut

Believe it or not, most employers aren't looking to hire people who are just going to go with the flow thoughtlessly. Hiring managers aren't looking for one-size-fits-all employees who follow or are easily influenced by others. The reason is that followers are lazy thinkers.

When you have lazy thinking skills, you may find taking the easy way out and letting others influence you convenient. Lazy thinkers make decisions without considering the best possible choices. They're like robots, doing exactly what they've been programmed to do and nothing more.

Lazy thinking is a work and life rut that's easy to fall into and hard to climb out of. You need to practice critical thinking skills, like those I discuss in the "Cultivating Core Critical Thinking Skills" section later in this chapter, every day.

All thinking begins with wondering.

—SOCRATES

Stepping on the critical thinking scale

Take a minute to reflect on your current critical thinking skills. Remember, the only right answers are your own. For each of the following statements, pick the answer that best describes you.

I use critical thinking daily in work and life situations.			
Always	Usually	Rarely	Never
I'm a naturally curious person.			
Always	Usually	Rarely	Never
I make informed decisions based on facts rather than personal opinion.			
Always	Usually	Rarely	Never
I find "going along to get along" easier at work and in life.			
Always	Usually	Rarely	Never
I ask myself what the problem is and why it exists before I try to solve it.			
Always	Usually	Rarely	Never
I generate a list of questions about the problem before I try to solve it.			
Always	Usually	Rarely	Never
I analyze a problem by looking for a cause-and-effect relationship before I implement a solution.			
Always	Usually	Rarely	Never

How did you weigh in on the critical thinking scale? If most of your responses are "always" or "usually," you're well on your way to being a successful critical and independent thinker! If most of your responses are "rarely" or "never," you've got some lazy thinking tendencies (see the preceding section), so cultivating your critical thinking skills is going to take a bit of work. The work is worth it, though, when you see how career- and life-changing critical thinking can be.

Discovery is seeing what everybody else has seen and thinking what nobody else has thought.

THE OBSTACLE IN THE PATH

In ancient times, a king had a boulder placed on a roadway. Then he hid himself and watched to see whether anyone would remove the huge rock. Some of the king's wealthiest merchants and courtiers came by and simply walked around it. Many loudly blamed the king for not keeping the roads clear, but none did anything about getting the big stone out of the way. Then a peasant came along carrying a load of vegetables. On approaching the boulder, the peasant laid down their burden and tried to move the stone to the side of the road. After much pushing and straining, they finally succeeded. As the peasant picked up their load of vegetables, they noticed a purse lying in the road where the boulder had been. The purse contained many gold coins and a note from the king indicating that the gold was for the person who thought of a way to remove the boulder from the roadway. The peasant learned what many others never understand: Every obstacle presents an opportunity to improve one's condition by thinking and acting independently.

Cultivating Core Critical Thinking Skills

Effective critical thinking requires the following five core skills, and each of them is essential to career and life success:

>> Thinking independently

>> Separating fact from opinion

>> Asking questions

>> Evaluating biases, assumptions, and perspectives

>> Being open minded and self-aware

Thinking independently

Successful critical thinkers develop their own points of view and independently make decisions based on their own findings. Surprisingly, thinking independently isn't always a solo act. Independent thinkers who work together as a team can often do wonders. They strengthen a team because they understand that different backgrounds and perspectives can generate different ideas and solutions. They can work together to brainstorm and combine their ideas into the best possible outcome for the whole group or organization.

Independent thinkers are willing to share ideas that differ from those of their fellow team members. When they view something as being wrong, they don't understand a situation, or they see a better way of doing something, independent thinkers have the confidence to voice their point of view.

Independent thinkers also share some common characteristics:

» They arrive at their own conclusions.

» They read — a lot.

» They gather information.

» They don't make decisions based on what others think.

» They think outside the box.

» They look at issues from all sides.

» They look for different ways to approach situations.

» They don't go with the flow just because everyone else is doing so; they turn the tide instead.

» They aren't afraid to be wrong.

» They know they can learn valuable lessons from making mistakes.

Separating fact from opinion

Critical thinkers know the difference between fact and opinion. Facts can be proven; opinions can't. When someone tells you their age, they're stating a fact. A quick look at their driver's license can prove it. But if the person goes on to say, "I look ten years younger than my age," they're stating a personal opinion.

Successful critical thinkers understand that opinions are personally biased and that they can be misleading at best and deceptive at worst. (Head to the later section "Evaluating bias, assumptions, and perspectives" for more on bias.) Many people get facts and opinions mixed up because determining which is which isn't always easy. Critical thinkers prefer to get just the facts first and let opinions slide. To separate the facts from opinions, critical thinkers ask questions, as I explain in the following section.

Asking questions

Good critical thinkers are always curious and constantly asking questions to understand and effectively deal with the world around them. Asking questions is an acquired adult skill, one that many people choose not to work on. Instead, they choose to simply accept what they see and what they're told without hesitation or consideration.

Using open-ended questions

TIP

One of the most important lessons journalists learn is how to conduct an interview to extract the most information possible from their subject. The first rule of interviewing is never to ask questions that require only a simple "yes" or "no" answer. Yes-or-no questions are *close-ended*, meaning they don't allow for any substantial information to be gathered. *Open-ended* questions are much more powerful and productive because they don't require such narrow answers.

Consider the following two questions:

» Do you think this plan is a good idea?

» What are your thoughts on this plan?

The first question calls for a simple yes-or-no answer while the second allows for a more detailed response. Bottom line: Ask better questions to get better answers with detailed information that can help you develop your point of view and an informed opinion in any situation.

Asking "why?"

Asking why questions is a soft skill that enhances the critical thinking process by helping you find out more about a person or situation. And you can apply this skill to every area of your life. Here's an exercise to help you get started. Answer each of the following questions and then ask yourself why you gave each response:

» What's your favorite thing to do on the weekend?

Why?

_____

_____

» Who do you like to spend time with?

Why?

_____

_____

» What's the hardest part of life?

Why?

_____

>> What causes you anxiety in your life?

Why?

_____

_____

>> What's your greatest hope for the future?

Why?

_____

_____

REMEMBER

As you can see from these examples, there's so much more to your story — and to every story — if you take the time to ask why.

Evaluating bias, assumptions, and perspectives

Biases, assumptions, and perspectives can influence how you read people and interpret situations and information. Successful critical thinkers are able to look at a question from another person's point of view without bringing their personal biases into play.

REMEMBER

Accepting others' perspectives is at the heart of critical thinking, and the way to do that is to ask the right questions to evaluate whether you have personal biases and make assumptions before accepting any new information as fact.

WARNING

Making assumptions can get you in trouble if you don't stop to question them. Assumptions aren't always wrong, but people often make them without having real proof that the assumptions are correct. Assumptions are often used to justify unfair treatment of others and are a barrier to critical thinking and problem solving.

Good critical thinking skills involve acknowledging your limitations and questioning your assumptions. One way to do so is by evaluating why you believe a particular thing to be true, as I discuss in the preceding section. But just because you have moments of prejudice or self-interested thinking doesn't mean you're not a great critical thinker. Being aware that you sometimes make assumptions about others based on your biases and perspectives is a great start to becoming a better and more successful critical thinker. Recognizing your biases is the first step to overcoming them and expanding your perspective.

Being open-minded and self-aware

The willingness to consider information that goes beyond your own experience and education — being *open-minded* — leads to becoming more self-aware. *Self-awareness* is the conscious knowledge of your own character, feelings, motives, and desires. A person who is self-aware isn't out to prove others wrong all the time and is willing to learn from and accept other points of view and new evidence. The goal of self-awareness is to pursue greater knowledge and understanding of the world around you.

Here's a quick way to gauge your current self-awareness. Try saying the following phrases aloud:

» I'm not perfect.

» I make mistakes.

» I can be wrong.

» If a situation calls for it, I'm perfectly willing and able to say, "Yes, I may be wrong. You may be right. I'm willing to change my mind when given good reasons."

Did some of the words get stuck in your throat? Were some of the phrases as foreign to you as a new language? If so, you can probably be more self-aware. Look for opportunities to change your thinking.

Being open minded and self-aware also means being on the lookout for reasonable and unreasonable behaviors — both from you and from others. Look at what's happening on the surface, but also look beneath the surface. Listen to what people say and closely examine their actions. Even if others don't think and act the way you do, ask yourself whether their views may have merit. See whether you can really hear what they're saying.

One of the hallmarks of a successful critical thinker is the ability to change one's mind when given a good reason. Being moved by reason is a sign someone is thinking for themselves. Still, many people are unwilling to change their way of thinking after their minds have been set; they're unwilling to listen or consider the views and opinions of those with whom they disagree.

Solving Problems Effectively

When you start thinking with a critical mind, you become a strategic problem solver. Problem solving means making choices and accepting their consequences, even when your choices don't turn out the way you want them to.

Having a road-map can help if your problem solving skills aren't particularly strong. The following nine steps to successful problem solving can help you find reasonable solutions to difficult situations:

1. **Identify the problem.**

If you can't recognize the problem, you can't solve it. Identify and describe the problem.

Example: I'm chronically late to work.

2. **Research the problem.**

Do your research. What's the history of the problem? How did it happen? Who's involved? What's the extent of the damage?

Example: I've stayed up late on my devices for years, and now it's become a habit. My roommate can stay up playing games and still wake up in the morning and get to work on time, but it's not working for me. I've already received two warnings from my manager; I've only got one warning left, and now I'm in danger of losing my job.

3. **Seek assistance.**

Find someone who can work with you to solve your problem.

Example: My roommate told me about a new alarm clock app that won't allow me to hit the snooze button.

4. **Make a hypothesis.**

Use creative thinking to envision a solution to the problem.

Example: I've heard that watching TV or playing games on your phone or tablet can stimulate your brain and keep you from sleeping. Maybe if I put away my devices (except the phone alarm) earlier, I'll fall asleep earlier and get up in the morning and make it to work on time more easily.

5. **Test your hypothesis.**

Put your solution into action and chart the results.

Example: I'll get off my devices an hour earlier each evening for one week to see what happens.

6. **Observe the results of your experiment.**

Did your experiment work? Has it been enough to completely solve your problem? If not, think about how you can change or add to your hypothesis.

Example: My brain was still pretty stimulated, and I wasn't able to fall asleep as quickly as I want. I did make it to work on time three mornings this week, but I want to do better.

7. Formulate a new plan.

Based on the results of your experimentation, make a plan for going forward.

Example: Turning off my devices at night is working, but I need to adjust the solution to make it more effective. I'll turn off my devices a full hour before I go bed and find ways to calm my brain at night. Maybe listening to music. Maybe breathing exercises.

8. Try out your new plan and learn from your mistakes.

You may need to try a few hypotheses before you find what works. Mistakes are good teachers. If you make one, find the lesson in it and try again! Then you can revise your theory and change your solution plan.

Example: Now I know I can't stay up late at night on my electronic devices, even listening to relaxing music, and still make it to work on time the next morning. But the breathing exercises have helped.

9. Examine your final results.

Take time to see what did and what didn't work with your plan. In the end, you should have a workable solution to the problem.

Example: Turning off the devices and doing breathing exercises equals a good night's sleep and a great on-time attendance record at work.

By continuing to develop your critical thinking skills, you're also developing your ability to redefine how you see the world around you. This skill improves your decision-making and problem-solving skills and gives you the tools you need to make the choices and decisions that are right for you — and best for the world around you.

Learn to use your brain power. Critical thinking is the key to creative problem solving in business.

—RICHARD BRANSON

Looking at Real-Life Scenarios: What Were They Thinking?

Two job applicants are preparing for their personal, on-ship interviews with a major cruise line. They're applying for the same position: cruise director. They've both made it through the tough application process and aced their human resources interviews. Tomorrow morning is their big chance to get onboard with this great company. But first, they have to meet the ship's captain, who has the final word.

» Getting it wrong: Job applicant one spends the evening watching reruns of the old 1970s and '80s television show *The Love Boat.* They figure they can learn everything they need to know for tomorrow from Julie, *The Love Boat's* fictional cruise director. Applicant one has also seen about a million cruise ship TV commercials, and they have only one question for the ship captain: How much shore leave does the cruise director get in each port? They're completely confident that they'll make a big splash tomorrow.

» Getting it right: Job applicant two spends the night researching the cruise line, digging deep into the website for information they can use the next day to show the captain they've done their homework. They've researched the ship they'll be working on and have taken a virtual tour. Applicant two has created a list of questions to ask the captain about the job, being part of a ship's crew, and being at sea. They're confident this is the position and the boat for them, and they're ready to prove it to the captain.

VOICES OF INDUSTRY

Stephanie Short

Vice President of Partnerships

America Succeeds

America Succeeds is a 501(c)(3) nonprofit founded in 2014 to engage business leaders in championing a modernized education system that creates opportunities for all learners to succeed. Its vision is for every student to succeed in the competitive global economy and contribute to their local community.

In an era when technical skills are evolving at an unprecedented pace, there is an important set of durable soft skills that last a lifetime. Durable skills include a combination of how you use what you know — skills like critical thinking, communication, collaboration, and creativity — and character skills like fortitude, growth mindset, and leadership. Durable skills are also known as soft skills, essential skills, employability skills, and 21st century skills.

(continued)

(continued)

America Succeeds partnered with Emsi Burning Glass to analyze more than 80 million job postings in 2019–2020 and 2020–2021 to quantify the demand for these skills. This report revealed that seven out of ten most requested skills in job postings are durable skills, with the leadership and communication competencies in the highest demand.

Also, the top five durable skills were requested in job postings 4.7 times more often than the top five hard skills. And 52.5 million job postings demanded durable skills across 22 occupational sectors. In short, durable skills are in high demand for jobs across the workforce, regardless of educational attainment level, industry, or geography.

Durable skills can make good employees great; we believe they are a requirement for success in every job. Better preparing learners and workers with these skills is not only a key part of economic recovery but also a powerful way to advance economic mobility and workforce diversity, equity, and inclusion.

Chapter **10**

Building a Strong Work Ethic

The harder you work to cultivate a good work ethic, the easier and more enjoyable any job gets. The internal and external rewards that come from working hard professionally lead to career and personal happiness and success.

In this chapter, you find out what having a good work ethic means and how to put that ethic to good use at your job and in your life. You also discover that working just a little bit harder isn't all that difficult, and that doing so can make achieving your goals much easier!

Opportunity is missed by most people because it is dressed in overalls and looks like work.

—THOMAS EDISON

Defining Work Ethic

Work ethic is the way you feel personally about the importance of work. Having a good or strong work ethic means you believe that hard work and diligence have a moral benefit and an inherent ability to strengthen character and enhance professional success. In other words, a good work ethic depends on believing in the importance of working hard. Work ethic is built on a set of values centered on the desire and determination to work hard.

REMEMBER

Your morals and values define you and help you know right from wrong. They're the foundation of who you are as an individual. Your work ethic determines and drives the way you approach the job, and the way you approach the job can help determine and drive your level of professional success.

You can't ignore the benefit of hard work. When you put your shoulder to the grindstone every day instead of thinking of work as a daily grind, you're going to get the job done well. The people you work with and for will likely notice your diligence, and that diligence contributes to your credibility and success.

I've come to believe that each of us has a personal calling that's as unique as a fingerprint — and that the best way to succeed is to discover what you love and then find a way to offer it to others in the form of service, working hard, and also allowing the energy of the universe to lead you.

—OPRAH WINFREY

Cultivating a Good Work Ethic

Contrary to popular opinion, most people aren't born with a good work ethic. It's a learned soft skill that needs cultivation over time. Watching others who value and prioritize hard work, such as family members, coaches, teachers, and employers, is the best way to develop a good work ethic in yourself.

Stepping on the work ethic scale

Read the following workplace statements and respond with never, rarely, usually, or always. If you don't currently have a job or haven't had a job yet, just apply the statements to your personal or school life. A good work ethic works everywhere!

I put in my best effort every day. When I say I'm going to do something, I do it.			
Never	Rarely	Usually	Always
I complete all my daily tasks to the best of my ability.			
Never	Rarely	Usually	Always

I know what I need to do every day and finish it without letting tasks pile up.			
Never	Rarely	Usually	Always

I set my own, higher productivity standards instead of relying on the company standards. I go the extra mile.			
Never	Rarely	Usually	Always

I work well with others and am happy to share both the work and the spotlight.			
Never	Rarely	Usually	Always

I'm 100 percent loyal to my co-workers, my company, and its rules. I can be trusted.			
Never	Rarely	Usually	Always

I'm honest when I've done a good job and when I make a mistake. I don't make excuses or try to blame someone else.			
Never	Rarely	Usually	Always

I don't depend on anyone or anything other than my inner drive and hard work for success.			
Never	Rarely	Usually	Always

I'm able to adapt to sudden and unexpected situations — both positive and negative. I can bend and not break.			
Never	Rarely	Usually	Always

If most of your responses are "usually" or "always," you're definitely headed in the right direction both personally and professionally. Keep up the good work ethic! If most of your responses are "rarely" or "never," get ready to put some work into your work ethic.

Knowing the ten work-ethic character traits

How can you spot someone who demonstrates a good work ethic, and how can you begin to foster one of your own? That's easy. All good work ethic role models share ten personal characteristics: discipline, reliability, dedication, productivity, cooperation, integrity, responsibility, professionalism, self-motivation, and flexibility.

Getting the job done with discipline

Perhaps the most important work ethic characteristic is discipline because none of the other nine characteristics can exist unless you have a superb level of discipline. Being *disciplined* means creating a schedule or plan and sticking to it by completing your daily tasks to keep your work moving forward. You can't allow work to pile up on your desk, because that leads to falling behind.

Relying on reliability

Simply put, *reliability* means, well, being dependable. It means being the kind of employee your colleagues and supervisors can trust to put in your best effort every time you show up. Having this work ethic characteristic signals that you can be counted on to do what's expected and needed, regardless of what you have going on behind the scenes.

Dedicating yourself to greatness

When you're truly dedicated to your job, you get down to it — no excuses. You complete your daily tasks to the best of your ability, no matter how hard the work is or how long it takes. Dedicated workers put extra effort into what they do, and they go the extra mile. They're dedicated to their own success and the success of the team, department, or company as a whole.

Setting your own productivity standards

The higher your level of productivity, the greater your chances of success. With some jobs, productivity standards are set by the company. If you're in that type of position, you should work to meet the standard, but you may want to push yourself to try to exceed it if you can do that without burning yourself out. You can also look for ways to contribute productively outside of meeting the company-established requirements of your position. Bonus: You may also motivate your colleagues by example.

TIP

Although it is important to work on your tasks until they are done and to give your best effort to meeting (or exceeding) productivity standards, working long or extra hours isn't a good criteria for measuring work ethic. You need to balance work and life while still demonstrating a positive work ethic. As I discuss in Chapter 7, there is a big difference between being busy and being productive. Make sure to manage your time wisely so that you're productive rather than just super busy or overworked.

Cooperating is key

You need to interact cooperatively with your colleagues and work supervisors. A spirit of cooperation is one of the most fundamental characteristics of a good work ethic because, believe it or not, some of the best work you do you accomplish through collaboration with similarly motivated colleagues. A competitive spirit may work on the sports field, but for general success in career and life, the old adage still stands: It's nice to share (both the work and the spotlight).

Having integrity

Integrity is a combination of honesty, loyalty, and reliability. Having integrity at work means you don't do anything wrong or potentially harmful to your colleagues or your employer's reputation. It means being loyal to your co-workers and to the company and its rules. People with integrity can be trusted. When you're trustworthy and have integrity, people know they can turn to you to help in difficult situations.

Taking responsibility

No employer on the planet wants to have an irresponsible employee on staff. Irresponsible employees can both undermine and compromise the interests and integrity of their colleagues and the company. Responsible employees are usually good leaders who excel at their work. They're also honest — meaning they not only take credit for good work successfully done but also tell the truth when they make mistakes or occasionally fail to produce as promised.

Practicing professionalism

Professionalism is behaving appropriately for the position you hold and the work environment. People who ace the professionalism work ethic characteristic dress, speak, and act in a manner that reflects their qualifications, experience, and skills. Professionalism is also about the way you accomplish your work. A professional pitches in to get the job done while making it both rewarding and fun.

Making it work with self-motivation

Self-motivation is all about jump-starting your work ethic motor every day from the inside out. A self-motivated person doesn't need someone else to tell them when to get out of bed, when to leave for work, and what to do while they're there. Without at least some self-motivation, succeeding at work and in life is impossible because motivation is a key component that helps you to rise above personal issues and prioritize keeping your eyes on the prize. Self-motivated people are rarely unsuccessful because they don't depend on anyone or anything else besides their own inner drive and hard work for success.

Being flexible

I'm not talking about being able to do the splits or an intricate yoga pose. In this case, flexibility means having the ability to adapt to sudden and unexpected situations (positive or negative). Flexible people can zig or zag; they don't have to walk only in a straight line. They can make exceptions to a rule when a situation requires it, and they can empathize. People with a good work ethic work hard, but they aren't rigid. They can bend, which is why they rarely break!

REMEMBER

Your level of success is determined only by your level of effort.

LIFE IS A DO-IT-YOURSELF PROJECT

An elderly carpenter was ready to retire. They told their employer of their plans to leave the house building business and live a more leisurely life with their spouse, enjoying their extended family. They'd miss the regular paycheck, but they'd get by. The contractor was sorry to see this good worker go and asked whether the carpenter would help build one more house as a personal favor.

The carpenter agreed, but it was clear to their soon-to-be-former employer that the builder's heart was no longer in the work. They resorted to shoddy work and used inferior materials. They just wanted the job done as quickly as possible.

When the house was finished and the contractor arrived to inspect it, they surprised the carpenter by handing over the key to the front door. "It's yours!" they said. "A thank-you gift for all the excellent work you've done for me for so many years."

What a shock! What a shame! If the carpenter had only known that they were building their own house, they would've done it all so differently. Now they were saddled with the substandard home they'd built for themself.

The moral of this story: If you build your life in a distracted way, reacting rather than acting, willing to put up less than your best, living with (or in) the substandard situations you create can be a real shock.

Think of yourself as the carpenter. Think about your dream house and your dream life. With every nail hammered, every board placed, every wall erected, you're designing your future success. This life is the only one you'll build. Do so wisely.

Putting a Good Work Ethic to Use

Having a good work ethic takes more than just possessing the characteristics I describe in the earlier section "Knowing the ten work-ethic character traits." You also have to apply those characteristics in a positive, productive, and professional way every day. In the following sections, I share five tips designed to help you do just that.

Embracing challenge

Everyone faces challenges from time to time. Life and work are easier when you acknowledge and embrace the fact that you'll most likely encounter daily challenges. One way to maintain a good work ethic in the face of challenges is to accept them as part of the job instead of flagging them as problems. The word *problem* suggests something is wrong or broken. Challenges are more like unsolved puzzles.

One important factor for being able to embrace challenge is keeping an open mind. Look for constructive ways to transform challenges into personal and professional development learning opportunities. When you welcome challenges head-on, the process of overcoming them becomes easier and easier over time, and your work ethic becomes better and stronger.

I have learned that success is to be measured not so much by the position that one has reached in life as by the obstacles which he has had to overcome while trying to succeed.

—BOOKER T. WASHINGTON

Taking accountability

Part of a good work ethic is taking accountability for your actions, your interactions with others, and the decisions and choices you make each day. You have to accept personal responsibility for your productivity — or lack thereof — and make a commitment to do a better job tomorrow than you may have done today.

One way you can keep yourself accountable is by taking a little accountability inventory at the end of each workweek. Give yourself pats on the back for jobs well done, note where you need improvement, and make a commitment to do better in those areas. Self-awareness goes hand in hand with accountability.

REMEMBER

Don't be upset by the results you didn't get with the work you didn't do. Instead, take the opportunity to improve in those areas.

Finding joy on the job

You may find maintaining a good work ethic hard if you're not having any fun in what you're doing. When work is joyless, it becomes drudgery, and that can truly mess with your motivation and work ethic maintenance.

TIP

If you're looking to find joy in your job and your life, try to gain a new perspective by looking at things through the eyes of your co-workers who seem to be taking joy in what they do. Ask them what brings them joy, and you just may find some renewed joy of your own.

Making habits a habit

Forming good habits is essential to the care and maintenance of a good work ethic. Repetition is the key to habits, so when you find a behavior that works well for you in the workplace or in life, practice doing it over and over and over again. Before you know it, you're doing it without even thinking about it, and your good habits are contributing to a good work ethic. Your self-motivation kicks in, and your productivity soars.

I am who I am today because of the choices I made yesterday.

—ELEANOR ROOSEVELT

Finding your inspiration

A good work ethic is based in self-awareness, a trait I discuss in Chapter 9. As with all soft skills, the strength of your work ethic comes down to you. If your life and career seem to lack meaning, reflect on what makes you happy. Decide what workplace and life happiness and success mean to you. Take an inventory of your strengths and your weaknesses, and identify the things that motivate you to work hard (for example, money, job satisfaction, climbing the corporate ladder, work-life balance, contributing to your team and community). Finally, and most importantly, ask yourself what you want most from life. When you know what you're seeking, you're more likely to find that passion and joy in your life.

TIP

Cultivating and maintaining a good work ethic are easy when you love what you do. So here's a bonus suggestion: After you've identified your inspiration, put your whole heart into it. When you truly put your heart into your work, everyone around you benefits.

Looking at Real-Life Scenarios: Loving It and Leaving It

Two produce clerks are nearing the end of their scheduled shift. Today, the produce truck was late, and although both clerks have been working diligently to get the fruits and vegetables restocked, they still have a few boxes to unpack. They're well within their rights to clock out and leave the unloaded produce in the back room. Their shift is over. A new crew arrives in the morning.

» **Getting it wrong:** The minute the shift ends, produce clerk one is out of there, despite the unpacked boxes and empty shelves. They untie their apron, hang it on a hook, and head for the time clock. This clerk has done the job for the day and earned their pay. And that's why they work: for the money. This clerk doesn't hate the job, but they don't love it, either. They clock in five days a week, do exactly what is required for the next eight hours — no less and no more — and then clock out. They never arrive one minute earlier and never leave one minute later. They don't have friends at work. As far as clerk one is concerned, this is just a job and a weekly paycheck, and they're doing just fine.

» **Getting it right:** Produce clerk two glances over as their co-worker hangs up their apron for the day. Clerk two could do the same. They've worked the same eight hours, and a few boxes won't make too much extra work for the morning crew. Then again, finishing the job won't take too much longer. This clerk knows how they feel when they arrive at the store to find extra work waiting. Besides, customers will be asking for the unpacked fruits and vegetables and will have to leave disappointed. Clerk two takes pride in having a fully stocked produce department and making sure everything is fresh. They love chatting with customers — especially the gardeners, because they're a gardener, too. They can talk fruits and vegetables all day long. As clerk one clocks out for the day, clerk two begins to unpack the last few boxes — not for praise or a raise but because it's their job. They truly enjoy what they do and believe doing a good job every day, no matter what it takes, is important. Today, because the truck was late, clerk two needs to go the extra mile, and they do it with a smile.

VOICES OF INDUSTRY

Stan Smith

Chairman

Stan Smith Events

Stan Smith is a former world-number-one tennis player. He founded Stan Smith Events in 1994 with Gary Niebur (President) with the mission to help companies entertain their most important partners and clients at major sporting events and conferences and the goal of helping them develop stronger relationships and trust and increase business. Stan Smith Events has worked at the four Grand Slam tennis events for the last 25 years, as well as the Rugby World Cup; the British Open; the Atlanta, Sydney, Salt Lake City, and London Olympics; and conferences at unique properties around the world. Its clients include several Fortune 100 companies.

The success of our company involves giving our clients and their guests access to special venues, celebrity interaction, unique activities, and premium signed memorabilia. The soft skills required to make our events work revolve around understanding the whole person and engaging their needs and desires. The activities we create use soft skills techniques to help break down the barriers and humanize the individuals so that they can relate better with each other and build stronger bonds.

These stronger relationships will ultimately lead to more trust, which is the key to long-term business success. Trust allows our company, our employees, and our clients to establish strong bonds and get more accomplished. Our 25 years of elite event success would not have been possible without teamwork, personal attention to each and every detail, and a dedication to creating exceptional experiences for our guests.

From the bottom of our organization to the top, soft skills make this happen. In order to take the best care of our clients, our people have to have great people skills. It is a show of respect to ensure that people are taken care of intentionally. It's a win-win for everyone when we work to help our clients and their guests understand each other's needs through clear communication, trust building practices, and an exemplary elite event experience.

IN THIS CHAPTER

» Getting a handle on what
leadership is

» Knowing the difference between big *L*
and little *l* leadership

» Leaving your leadership legacy

Chapter 11

Leading from Anywhere in the Organization

Although leaders sometimes achieve their position through family legacy, in many cases, leaders are 100 percent self-made. The process of becoming a leader starts on the inside; you have to be able to lead yourself before you can lead others. Over time, with practice and perseverance, a person begins to gain recognition as a leader from the people around them

REMEMBER

Successful leaders lead by example. When you're committed to living a life of integrity and have cultivated a strong set of leadership skills on the inside, you're well on your way to becoming a leader on the outside.

In this chapter, I explain what leadership looks like, the different types of leaders, the essential soft skills that lead to personal and professional leadership success, and how to create your own leadership legacy.

REMEMBER

You *manage* things; you *lead* people.

Defining Leadership

Every day, life offers opportunities for you to make a difference in the lives of others through leadership, and you can demonstrate your leadership skills in many ways. You can be a good leader without being the boss or having an important job title.

The kind of leadership I'm talking about has to do with bringing out the best in yourself and others. It's about acting and communicating with clear intention, expressing your beliefs in a way that represents your unique views, and being a model in the way you live your life.

Stepping on the leadership scale

Before you can lead others — and before they'll follow your lead — you must first believe in yourself. A leader is effective because of who they are on the inside and how those qualities are reflected on the outside.

Who are you? What do you care about? How can you make a difference? Your answers to these questions and the work you do to acquire the new skills to address them are what make up your leadership potential.

Take a few minutes to see where you are today so you know whether you're setting a positive leadership example in the workplace and in life or you need to work on improving some skills. Read each of the following statements and rate your leadership skills (with 1 being "not like me at all" and 5 being "exactly like me").

I believe others consider me to be a strong team player.				
1	2	3	4	5
I'm always striving to improve and find ways to perform my job better.				
1	2	3	4	5
I love my job and bring lots of energy and enthusiasm to it each day.				
1	2	3	4	5
I don't blame others, and I always accept responsibility for my actions.				
1	2	3	4	5
I'm constantly trying new approaches, learning, and changing.				
1	2	3	4	5

I'm organized, consistent, and dependable.				
1	2	3	4	5
I communicate openly and honestly with teammates.				
1	2	3	4	5
I listen with an open mind and genuinely try to hear others.				
1	2	3	4	5
I have an attitude of gratitude that I openly demonstrate to others.				
1	2	3	4	5
I show up on time and ready to get to work.				
1	2	3	4	5

Remember, this quiz is simply a way for you to get an idea of where you currently stand on the leadership scale; it's just the beginning of your leadership journey. Add up the values of your responses to each statement and then check your results against this scoring system:

>> 40–50 points: You're on your way to becoming a leader that others want to follow!

>> 26–39 points: You're getting there. Keep striving and working toward your goals.

>> 10–25 points: You have some leadership skills work to do.

Leaders are originals, not duplicates.

Knowing what a leader looks like

You don't have to have a special set of talents to take a leadership role in your life. You're special just as you are. You can share your unique leadership qualities simply by being your best you regardless of whether you're managing a work crew, coaching a local sports team, becoming a parent, or coordinating a block party in your neighborhood.

The idea that only a lucky few can lead is a myth. Many kinds of leaders and ways to lead exist, but they all require a certain set of soft skills to bring about workplace and life success. When I list my ten essential soft skills, leadership comes last for a reason: The other nine are the building blocks to leadership. Take a look at each of those nine skills (which I cover in more detail in other chapters) and how they apply to leadership:

>> **Attitude (Chapter 2):** Attitude is everything to be a successful leader. In other words, you may be good at what you do and have the best hard skill set of any employee in the company, but your attitude is what makes you a standout in the workplace and attracts positive attention and opportunities for promotion and leadership.

>> **Character (Chapter 3):** Your thoughts, words, and actions all come together to create your character. Displaying good character in the workplace can help you achieve consistent on-the-job success. Good employers promote employees with good character. They give them pay raises and company awards. They put them in leadership positions.

>> **Communication (Chapter 4):** To be a leader, you have to be able to communicate clearly. Leaders excel at the many different ways of communicating. When you can communicate effectively and positively on all levels, you gain the confidence of co-workers and customers, and your career leadership opportunities soar.

>> **Respecting diversity and developing cultural awareness (Chapter 5):** As you step out of your current community and into a culturally diverse workplace, you'll be standing side by side with all kinds of people from all kinds of places. Some may even bring new customs and beliefs into the workplace with them. You don't have to embrace others' beliefs, but if you want to be considered for promotion and an eventual leadership position, you have to recognize, respect, and respond positively to cultural differences, otherwise known as diversity, within your organization.

>> **Appearance and manners (Chapter 6):** Leaders look and act the part of being a leader. They're careful with their appearance, and they use good manners to treat others with respect. Co-workers and colleagues look up to leaders and often model their clothing, attitudes, and behaviors. The impression you make, positive or negative, when you first meet someone is primarily based on your appearance and etiquette, especially if you aspire to a leadership position.

>> **Time management (Chapter 7):** It's a rule of workplaces everywhere: To be functional, you must be punctual. In today's fast-paced working world, showing up on time just isn't enough, especially if you want to be recognized as a leader. Leaders manage their time; they don't let time manage them. They make the most of every single minute of every single day.

>> **Teamwork (Chapter 8):** Successful businesses rely on employees who can work with each other rather than against one another. The best and most

successful leaders are also the best team players. They lead by example, not by being bossy. They jump right in and do whatever is necessary to help the team get the job done.

» **Critical thinking (Chapter 9):** Training your mind to think critically and solve problems effectively carries you far in the workplace. Using your head in a positive and productive way can make all the difference in peak job performance and promotion and leadership opportunities. Do you look at problems with an open mind? Are you good at coming up with creative solutions to sticky situations? The better you become at solving problems, the more confident you can be in dealing with your daily work responsibilities.

» **Work ethic (Chapter 10):** Leaders have excellent work ethics. They work hard, and then they work a little harder. They go the extra mile. They love what they do and they give it their all. Co-workers naturally look up to them. Employers want to make sure they stay with the company, so they put them in leadership positions and provide incentives to show appreciation for the hard work.

REMEMBER

Successful leaders lead by example. When you're committed to living a life of integrity and have cultivated a strong set of leadership skills on the inside, you're well on your way to becoming a leader on the outside.

Sizing Up Leadership Skills

An Internet search of the word *leadership* offers more than 3 billion results. That's a lot of leads on the subject! In this section, I explore just two types of leadership skills I call big *L* and little *l*.

Leading with the big L

You demonstrate *big L leadership* by literally leading others — that is, being in charge. These leaders make the laws and the big calls. They spend a lot of time in the spotlight and live big lives.

Not everyone is cut out — or wants — to be a big *L* leader. According to a research survey by the Wilson Learning Corporation, the ten reasons people most often give for choosing big *L* leader careers are

» Glory

» Power

>> Respect

>> Recognition

>> Prestige

>> Control

>> Personal duty

>> Self-fulfillment

>> Challenge

>> Money

A common thread runs through those ten responses. Almost every single one has to do with wanting some sort of personal gain. But that's not necessarily a bad thing. You can want personal gain and still be a good person who cares about others.

REMEMBER

The world needs big *L* leaders. It needs heads of state, legislators, and corporate CEOs who lead companies, employ workers, and provide the products people need to live. And not every big *L* leader is looking for power and money and glory. Many big *L* leaders genuinely care about others and want to serve their communities. The best leaders can do both.

Leading with the little l

You demonstrate *little l leadership* quietly through your everyday actions and interactions with others — by the way you influence and affect the lives of those around you. Demonstrating little *l* leadership characteristics on the outside helps you build a strong self-leadership foundation on the inside, preparing you for success in everything you do.

Take a few minutes and think about someone in your personal or professional life whose leadership has influenced you. How has this person demonstrated leadership? Feel free to make a list of the qualities on a piece of scratch paper.

Now compare your description to the following little *l* leadership qualities:

>> Has my best interest in mind

>> Helps me through rough spots

>> Is committed to a goal

>> Is open and caring

>> Is open minded

>> Knows my unique abilities

>> Challenges me

>> Keeps my spirits up

>> Keeps me on track

>> Knows what they're doing

>> Has confidence in me

>> Is supportive

>> Makes time for me

>> Is confident

How did your description of your personal leader match up to this list? My guess is that it includes at least a few of these same little *l* leadership qualities. And it probably doesn't mention any of the big *L* leadership qualities from the preceding section.

Little *l* leadership qualities and big *L* leadership qualities aren't the same things. Where big *L* leadership is typically motivated by personal gain and power, little *l* leadership is more about giving and empowering than receiving something and exercising power over others.

REMEMBER

Despite the lowercase letter, little *l* leaders — those who choose to empower others rather than seek power — often become very powerful and successful people. They inspire. They make a positive difference in the world and in the lives of others.

Creating a Leadership Legacy

A leader is best when people barely know he exists, when his work is done, his aim fulfilled, they will say: we did it ourselves.

—LAO TZU

Everyone leaves a legacy. Each person is remembered for something they did — or didn't do. What kind of personal and professional legacy do you want to leave? How do you want people to remember you? What do you want them to say?

Leadership legacy is the sum total difference you make in people's lives directly, indirectly, formally, informally, personally, and professionally. You create your leadership legacy by how you choose to live each day, both at work and in life in general. Your leadership legacy is made up of the memories, positive and negative, that you leave behind after every action and interaction in your day.

REMEMBER

Legacy leaders understand that actions and behaviors matter more than many people realize. They know that everything they do, as well as all the things they don't do, plays a role in determining their success.

Each day, you have countless opportunities to make a positive difference in the world around you. Today's opportunity may come during a conversation with a co-worker or friend, during a company meeting, after school while you're on the soccer field with your teammates, or tonight at the dinner table with your family.

The point is that no matter where you are or when, you get to decide what kind of impact you want to make. When you choose not to make a positive difference, you almost always make a negative one. By choosing to make a positive difference in the lives of others today, you increase your chances for professional success and personal satisfaction tomorrow!

It's never too early — or too late — to start considering your life, your future, and your leadership legacy. Thinking today about how you want to be remembered tomorrow can be a powerful motivator. Deciding whether you want to be someone who leads by empowering others or someone who simply exercises power charts your future career and life course.

Looking at Real-Life Scenarios: Taking the Lead

A team leader position has just opened at a large mail order catalog company, and the company president is trying to decide which of two potential candidates should get the position. Both employees have a strong set of soft skills and have successfully put them into action on the job. They're equal in terms of attitude, character, appearance and etiquette, time management, cultural awareness, critical thinking and problem solving, teamwork, and work ethic How they use those skills when put in a leadership position is a completely different story.

>> **Getting it wrong:** Candidate one arrives to lead their first shift, determined to show the company president that they have what it takes to be a leader. They start by making sure their co-workers know they're now a boss, not a buddy. No more friendly chat while they're filling orders, no jumping in to help team members reach their daily fulfillment quotas. Nope. Candidate one is all about being a bossy, big *L* leader now. They're too busy trying to impress the company president, tossing out orders in a power-crazed frenzy, to even notice that their overpowered team members have lost energy, enthusiasm, and effectiveness. But the company president notices and isn't the least bit impressed.

>> **Getting it right:** Candidate two arrives to lead their later shift that afternoon, determined to show the company president that they're ready to do everything in their power to be a good leader by empowering their co-workers to be the best they can be individually and as a team. They find something complimentary to say to each team member during the shift and are always ready to jump in and lend a hand when needed. Candidate two understands that a team leader's job is to make sure that the team works, so they do whatever they need to to make everyone on the team look good. This candidate most definitely has the look of a leader — a little *L* leader who leads by example. The company president definitely notices this promise and is quite impressed.

You can read more about big and little *L* leadership in the earlier section "Sizing Up Leadership Skills."

VOICES OF INDUSTRY

Madeline Pumariega

President

Miami Dade College

Madeline Pumariega is the first female president leading one of the nation's largest educational institutions, Miami Dade College (MDC). In her role, she has prioritized strong partnerships and is working with businesses to identify the skills key industries need, tailor higher education programs that match those demands, and ensure each MDC graduate is workforce ready. Known as democracy's college, Miami Dade College changes lives through accessible, high-quality teaching and learning experiences and embraces its responsibility to serve as an economic, cultural, and civic leader for the advancement of the diverse global community.

(continued)

(continued)

Technological innovations, new industries, and fluctuations in the economy bring about unprecedented, fast-paced changes in the global job market. These disruptions may exacerbate skills gaps among workers competing for jobs in a highly competitive, dynamic, and evolving workforce.

What remains constant are the expectations of employers to hire staff who are excellent communicators and collaborators, critical thinkers, and problem solvers. Employers are looking to retain individuals who are resilient, adaptive, ethical, culturally competent, and focused on the advancement of the company goals as well as on their professional growth. These foundational skills are also known as "soft skills" — universal enterprise skills evident in the work performance of everyone.

As the future of work transitions from traditional establishments into on-demand work opportunities, soft skills are key for individuals to thrive in the changing workplace. The future of work is less daunting when educational institutions adopt new teaching and learning models, designed for early acquisition of a growth mindset and continuous development of soft skills — embedded in high-quality programs aligned with technical training specific to industry demands.

While we cannot predict what jobs will exist in the future economy, we can predict that soft skills are futureproof. Why? Because the transferability of these skills from one occupation or industry to another allows for an employee to adapt successfully even when their sector has been impacted by disruptive change. Any individual who adopts these practices is poised to remain competitive and resilient in securing a job in the future.

3
Applying Soft Skills in Specific Situations

Use soft skills in social and other nonwork settings.

Impress prospective employers with your soft skills.

Chapter **12**

Bringing Your Soft Skills to Life

S oft skills are sometimes referred to as *life skills* because they're tools you can use every day to create a powerful, positive, and productive life. The road to professional success starts with the path to personal success, and cultivating a strong set of soft skills can go a long way to making both happen.

In this chapter, I explain how to bring each of the ten critical soft skills to your life and why doing so is essential to success and life happiness.

Taking Soft Skills Personally

Attitude, character, communication, cultural awareness, appearance and etiquette, time management, critical thinking, work ethic, and leadership. Each of these soft skills contributes to how you see yourself and others and how you perceive and comprehend the world around you. Building a strong set of soft skills is important to becoming not only a better and happier employee but also a better and happier person in general.

REMEMBER

Before you take your soft skills to work, you have to know how to make them work for you personally. Using your soft skills with your friends and family makes you the kind of person other people want to spend time with. People who don't have personal soft skills lack

>> The emotional intelligence to read a room

>> The integrity to be honest

>> Empathy in situations where they could've demonstrated kindness

>> The consideration to be on time for family and social functions

>> Enthusiasm for others' success

>> The motivation to work hard at relationships

>> The ability to be a team player

>> The skill-set to resolve conflict

>> Approachability and an open mind

>> The ability to handle stressful situations

>> Positivity

>> Problem-solving skills and perspective

>> Discipline and self-control

>> The ability to think of anyone other than themselves

If you don't have these soft skills necessary to keep your personal relationships mutually beneficial or if you don't nurture those relationships, you can get fired as a friend just as you can get fired from a job.

You've probably had a friend with whom things just didn't work out, right? For example, maybe you gave up on someone when they let you down. No one wants to be around someone they can't count on, and being a dependable friend or relative requires strong soft skills. Maybe you've known someone who tends to get in verbal disputes at social gatherings, complains all the time, or acts selfishly. These types of issues are just a few of the many soft skills problems that you may encounter in everyday life.

Making an inventory of your values

Getting in touch with your authentic self means getting to know who you are and what your values are. Your *personal values* consist of the things that you consider most important in life. When you consciously identify your values, you can create a plan to set yourself on a path to living life as your authentic self and achieving the goals that are important to you.

To identify what you value most, take a look at the following 20 life values. Consider each to decide whether it's extremely important, kind of important, or not at all important to you. There's no right or wrong answer. The goal is for you discover what you value so you can begin to create a plan for your life that brings you personal and professional happiness and fulfillment.

Wisdom: Having mature understanding, insight, good sense, and good judgment		
Extremely important	Kind of important	Not important

Wealth: Having many possessions and plenty of money for the things I want		
Extremely important	Kind of important	Not important

Trustworthiness: Being honest, straightforward, and caring		
Extremely important	Kind of important	Not important

Religion/faith: Having religious belief		
Extremely important	Kind of important	Not important

Recognition: Being important, well-liked, and accepted		
Extremely important	Kind of important	Not important

Power: Having control, authority, or influence over others		
Extremely important	Kind of important	Not important

Pleasure: Having satisfaction, gratification, fun, and joy		
Extremely important	Kind of important	Not important

Physical appearance: Being attractive, neat, clean, and well-groomed		
Extremely important	Kind of important	Not important

Morality: Believing in and keeping ethical standards, personal honor, and integrity		
Extremely important	Kind of important	Not important

Loyalty: Maintaining allegiance to a person, group, or institution		
Extremely important	Kind of important	Not important

Loyalty: Exhibiting warmth, caring, unselfish devotion		
Extremely important	Kind of important	Not important
Knowledge: Seeking truth or information for satisfaction or curiosity		
Extremely important	Kind of important	Not important
Justice: Treating others fairly or impartially; conforming to truth, fact, or reason		
Extremely important	Kind of important	Not important
Honesty: Being frank and genuine with everyone		
Extremely important	Kind of important	Not important
Health: Taking care of my body and physical condition		
Extremely important	Kind of important	Not important
Creativity: Being innovative and developing new ideas and designs		
Extremely important	Kind of important	Not important
Job: Being proud of my lifetime work		
Extremely important	Kind of important	Not important
Family: Taking care of my present/future family		
Extremely important	Kind of important	Not important
Education: Pursuing school, college, or trade school		
Extremely important	Kind of important	Not important
Achievement: Accomplishing results through resolve, persistence, or endeavor		
Extremely important	Kind of important	Not important

Knowing what's important to you makes you a happier person and a happier employee. When your personal interests and values are well-matched with the people in your life, you increase your chances for success and genuine happiness. And job satisfaction increases when you're doing something that interests you and that you consider important.

TIP

After you've identified which values are most important to you, keep those values in mind when you're making important life decisions. Consider the following questions as part of your decision-making process:

- » Is this important to me?

- » Do I feel good about this being important to me?

- » Would I feel good if people I respect knew that this was important to me?

- » Have I ever done anything that indicates this is important to me?

- » Is this a decision I'd stand by even if others made fun of me for it?

- » Does this decision fit in with my dream vision of who I am?

Zeroing in on your core values

Believe it or not, your behavior always follows your beliefs because your beliefs, and what you do and don't personally value, pattern your behavior.

TIP

If you haven't already gone through the personal value inventory in the preceding section, do so now. Make a list of all the values you consider extremely important. This group is your list of *core life values* — the things that are most important to you for making important life choices and living your happiest and best life, both personally and professionally.

Find a prominent place for your list — somewhere you'll be sure to see it at least once a day. Tape it to your refrigerator or your bathroom mirror or keep it in your wallet so it's always handy when you need to make a life decision in a hurry and you're not sure which way to go. Eventually, checking your list will become a habit, which is an important part of becoming the best version of yourself.

Incorporating Soft Skills into Your Daily Life

Soft skills don't just come into play when you clock into your job each day. Using soft skills 24/7, 365 in all areas of your life is important, and no one skill is more important than another because they all work together for overall soft skill success. In this section, I discuss each of the ten soft skills and provide a common scenario that will show how they can be impactful and valuable to your everyday life.

Getting into character with attitude

Your *attitude* (how you choose to see your life) strengthens your *character* (how you choose to live your life). You may know someone who always chooses to see the glass as half empty, and you may not find that person much fun to be around. People want to be around people who have a positive attitude about life and their work. Employers want to hire and promote positive people.

>> **The scenario:** You and a group of friends are meeting for dinner before a concert. Everyone decides to try out a new Thai restaurant. Thai isn't your kind of thing, and you aren't happy about the group's choice.

>> **Putting your skills to work:** You could complain and try to get the group to choose a different restaurant — and bring down the happy mood of the evening. Instead, you practice the soft skills of attitude and character by deciding to be willing to try something new and find the item on the menu that appeals to you most.

I discuss attitude and character in Chapters 2 and 3, respectively.

Communicating by listening

Knowing how to effectively communicate with others is essential. Speaking your mind is one part of the successful communication equation, but equally important is the ability to listen as well as, if not better than, you speak. If you aren't an active listener, having empathy for others can be difficult, and your family and social relationships can suffer.

>> **The scenario:** A friend calls in a panic. Their aged, single mom isn't doing well living on her own, and your friend is going through the hard decision process of whether to move her into a long-term senior care facility.

>> **Putting your skills to work:** You don't know the mother or much about long-term care facilities, and you really have a lot of other things to do, so you're tempted to listen halfheartedly. However, you'd be letting your friend down by doing that. But you know that sometimes people just need to say what's on their minds even if the person they're talking to can't provide a solution, so you employ the soft skill of effective communication and active listening to allow your friend to share their fears and concerns about the situation.

Chapter 4 has more info on communication.

Respecting diversity and culture

Imagine a world where people aren't open to new or different ideas and where everyone lived exactly the same life. What a boring and unimaginative place this planet would be! As I explain in Chapter 5, widening the circle to let everyone in is an important skill because successful people are inclusive rather than exclusive.

>> **The scenario:** It's your child's seventh birthday, and you're hosting a circus party in your backyard.

>> **Putting your skills to work:** Rather than invite the entire second grade class, you could send your child to school with invitations for only the kids you know they play with at recess — kids who are just like them and who have parents who are just like you. Those invited will be delighted, but those not invited will be devastated, and you're able to accommodate everyone. So instead you respect diversity and culture and decide to give your child an important life lesson by inviting all members of the class.

Looking and acting the part

In Chapter 6, I explain how people typically form an instant, and often lasting, first impression of you after only four seconds. What are you showing the world every day with your personal appearance and etiquette (manners)? Happy people look and act the part.

>> **The scenario:** Your boss pops their head into your office and asks if you're available to drive them to pick up their car at the repair center. You agree, but as you click the unlock button on your car's key fob, you remember that you don't keep the most presentable car.

>> **Putting your skills to work:** Even beyond the four-second first impression, your appearance and etiquette can influence what others think of you. Your office, cubicle, lunch area, and even car can contribute to a positive or negative impression. Take time to care for your surroundings.

Managing your time

Sure, life is busy, but it's busy for everyone. When you aren't punctual, you're telling others that your time is more valuable than theirs. You have to be disciplined about managing your time. Happy people make time work for them by being proactive about their schedules rather than reactive, and they usually seem to have plenty of time to enjoy life.

>> **The scenario:** You and your sister have a standing lunch date every third Monday. You're usually 10 to 15 minutes late, and your sister expects and excuses this tardiness. She grew up with you, after all. Today, you're almost 30 minutes late; you've been too busy running around (because you lost track of time) to shoot your sister a text to let her know you were going to be really late. When you arrive at the restaurant, the owner tells you that your sister left five minutes ago.

>> **Putting your skills to work:** Instead of always expecting your sister to wait on you, you resolve to turn over a new leaf. The next day you have lunch planned, you set your alarm clock 15 minutes earlier than normal, make sure your morning schedule is free of any obligations that are likely to run longer than you anticipate, and plan to arrive at the restaurant 5 minutes before the appointed time.

I cover time management in Chapter 7.

Teaming up

People like to be around people with a collaborative spirit. Employers like employees who work well with others and can foster a healthy team environment. Good team players don't need to always be in the spotlight. The more you can practice working as a team in your daily life experiences and routine, the better teammate you are in the workplace.

>> **The scenario:** You play on a weekend intramural softball team at the local community center. Just as Saturday's game is about to begin, you and your teammates learn that your captain — and best player — has a sick child at home and can't make the game.

>> **Putting your skills to work:** Your captain usually plays shortstop, a position you're also talented at but hate playing. You'd much rather take your normal role in left field, but with the captain out, you volunteer to fill in at shortstop because you know it's best for the team.

Flip to Chapter 8 for details on teamwork as a soft skill.

Putting on your (critical) thinking cap

Problem solvers get things done! They know how to multitask and think creatively. Many people juggle a lot: work, kids, community volunteerism, personal hobbies, adult education, and more. The ability to think calmly and critically in everyday life situations can help you meet problems and situations head on and solve them effectively.

>> **The scenario:** You have an appointment you just can't miss, and you're ready to go (with some time to spare) when you discover you have a flat tire.

>> **Putting your skills to work:** You can give up and decide that you just need to call to cancel the appointment (which may give the person you're meeting a bad impression), or you can apply your critical thinking skills to come up with an alternative solution, such as by calling a friend or family member for a ride, taking public transportation, or using a ride-share app.

Chapter 9 has the skinny on critical thinking.

Work ethic

People with a good work ethic don't apply that work ethic only to their employment. They also bring it to their daily duties to keep their lives running smoothly. They're happy to get the job done. When the job is done, they're happy to have fun because they know they've earned it. Hard-working people often have lots of friends and professional opportunities because they're responsible, reliable, and respected.

>> **The scenario:** You have a job to do: cleaning the kitchen in the apartment you share with two roommates. It's not an especially fun job, but it's your turn to do it.

>> **Putting your skills to work:** You could do the job halfway. Your roommates probably even won't notice the place isn't spotless when they get home from their lunch shifts at the restaurant where you all wait tables. They'll be tired, and you won't be there when they get home because you work the dinner shift. Then again, you know how nice it is to come home from a long night waiting tables to find the kitchen tidy. Think how good returning the favor and seeing the smiles on their faces will feel. As you pull out the cleaning supplies, your good work ethic really kicks in, and you decide to also wash everyone's towels and sheets to make things a little extra special for your roommates.

Read more about work ethic in Chapter 10.

Leading the way to a satisfying life

As I discuss in Chapter 11, some people are big L leaders, and some are little l leaders in life. Big L leaders live large by leading people, companies, and countries. Little l leaders live by example to influence those closest to them.

>> **The scenario:** You've been chosen to lead the committee for the neighborhood's annual block party. This party is a big deal, and being chosen to lead

the committee is an even bigger deal. You want to make sure both you and the party are a big success. The committee has five other members, and although they're happy and eager to help, all of them have ideas about how to make this the best block party ever.

>> **Putting your skills to work:** You can be a big *L* leader and step into the spotlight to take command of the situation and delegate responsibilities. You can be a little *l* leader, listening to, embracing, and encouraging each committee member's ideas. The best option, though, is to exercise both types of leadership. Work with the other committee members to select the best of all the ideas offered and then divide and conquer by delegating responsibilities for putting the ideas into action.

Happiness is not a goal. It's a by-product of a life well-lived.
—ELEANOR ROOSEVELT

SEEKING HAPPINESS

Two hundred people are attending a seminar on mental and physical health. The speaker gives each attendee a balloon and a marker and tells them to write their name on their balloon. The balloons are collected and moved into a very small room. The participants are instructed to go into the small room and find their balloons within two minutes.

What happens next? Chaos.

People search frantically for their balloons, pushing each other and running into one another while grabbing balloons, looking at them, and tossing them in the air when they don't see their names. When the two-minute bell rings to signal the end of the activity and the seminar participants reenter the auditorium, not one person is holding a balloon.

The speaker smiles and asks the participants to go back into the smaller room, pick a balloon at random, and find its owner. Within minutes, everyone has been reunited with their original balloon.

The speaker smiles again. "This is what it's like when people are frantically searching for their own life happiness. They push others aside to get the things that they believe will bring them happiness. However, happiness actually lies in helping other people and working together as a community."

Chapter **13**

Showing Off Your Soft Skills to Prospective Employers

ard skills demonstrate your *aptitude* — your ability to do the job. Soft skills demonstrate your *attitude* — your ability to work with others and grow within a company. Soft skills not only make the hard skills work but also take the hard skills to work because more and more employers are hiring for attitude and training for aptitude. Listing soft skills on your resume and demonstrating them in the interview give potential employers a better idea of the kind of person you are and the kind of employee you can be one day.

In this chapter, I explain how to best present yourself to prospective employers on paper. I also cover how to demonstrate your soft skills when you have the opportunity to for an in-person interview.

Preparing to Get a Job that Fits You

Before you put your soft skills to work to help you get — and keep — the job of your dreams, you should consider exactly what that dream job may look like. Being aware of your career path personality makes your job search much easier and more individually directed.

The *RIASEC model*, also known as the *Holland Code*, determines your career personality type and is a successful predictor for finding happiness in a career. According to the model, people fall into six main career personality groups: realistic, investigative, artistic, social, enterprising, and conventional.

>> **Realistic** career personality types are doers, which include people who prefer to work with objects, machines, tools, plants, or animals rather than ideas. Realistic personality types often have athletic or mechanical ability and like to be outdoors. They like concrete problems with clear answers and are drawn toward structure and order when working with people.

>> **Investigative** career personality types are problem solvers, which include people who like to observe, learn, investigate, analyze, evaluate, or solve problems (primarily scientific or mathematical ones). People with this personality type prefer working with ideas rather than people, and they like open-ended problems with multiple solutions.

>> **Artistic** career personality types are creators, which include people who like to use their imagination and creativity to make things. They tend to be inventive, original, perceptive, sensitive, and independent. They don't like rules and structure and prefer instead to think outside the box.

>> **Social** career personality types are helpers, which include people who like to work with other people to inspire, inform, help, train, or cure them. People with this personality type prefer to solve problems by talking to people. They tend to be drawn to seeking close relationships with other people and are less likely to want to engage in activities that are primarily intellectual or physical.

>> **Enterprising** career personality types are persuaders, which include people who like to work with other people to influence, manage, and lead them, usually for an organization or business. They tend to be good talkers, and they may also like to take on big projects and achieve big organizational or financial goals.

>> **Conventional** career personality types are organizers, which include people who like to work with data, are good with numbers, and enjoy carrying things out in detail or following others' instructions. They typically like working indoors and at tasks that involve organizing and being accurate. They're most comfortable in structured situations rather than open-ended ones.

TIP

If you don't already know which personality group you fall into, take the Holland Code survey, such as the one at Open-Source Psychometrics Project (http://openpsychometrics.org/tests/RIASEC/) to determine your career personality or RIASEC score.

After you have the results of the survey, compare them to the list of career personality types. Does your highest RIASEC theme feel like a good fit?

TIP

When browsing through job application sites or the want ads section of your local paper, look for jobs that suit your career path personality. If none of the preceding personality type descriptions seems like it matches you, take a little time to read through the list again. Look at the specific things each personality type likes to do and see whether any of them applies to you. You can also show your Holland Code survey results to someone whose opinion you trust and ask them which career personality type they think best suits you.

Applying Soft Skills to the Hiring Process

Employers recognize the importance of soft skills in the workplace, so you can try to attract notice by putting soft skills at the forefront of your resume and job applications.

The following are some reasons promoting your soft skills catches employers' and hiring managers' eyes:

>> **Indicating longevity:** When hiring for a position, most employers look for signs that an applicant will stay at their company for the long term. Demonstrating that you understand the importance of having a strong work ethic both on the job and in life can make you attractive to potential employers. You can read more about work ethic in Chapter 10.

>> **Measuring teamwork:** If you're applying for a position as part of a team, the hiring manager judges your application partly based on how well you can fit into a group dynamic. Potential employers need people who can contribute to a team environment, so they want to know whether you have the skills needed to be a good team player. To bone up on those skills, check out Chapter 8.

>> **Maintaining relationships:** Soft skills not only support your relationships with others in the workplace but also determine your success working with clients and business partners. Employers seek out employees they can trust to represent the company in a professional and friendly way. Soft skills

differentiate between candidates who are qualified for a job and candidates who will exceed expectations by putting effort into their professional relationships.

>> **Facilitating growth:** Soft skills contribute to your ability to make the most of your existing hard skills set, and they also help you develop and grow within the company. Employers want to hire people who demonstrate their understanding of soft skills by constantly and consistently looking for ways to improve their job performance and the success of the organization.

>> **Staying organized:** Attention to detail, time management (see Chapter 7), and the ability to delegate are soft skills that determine how organized you are at work. Being organized helps you prove that you're a reliable resource who can do your work well and in a timely manner. You can demonstrate your organizational skills to potential employers by communicating promptly and submitting a well-formatted resume.

>> **Proving initiative:** Employers hire and promote people who regularly demonstrate motivation and initiative. Having a positive attitude and being creative shows employers that you have the initiative to think of new projects or ways to solve problems. Emphasize your soft skills to show potential employers that you have plans to grow and inspire others through your focus and drive.

>> **Gaining confidence:** Your social skills can help you navigate workplace issues with confidence. This trait can be especially useful during the interview, where your confidence in your soft skills may convince an employer to choose you over another applicant.

REMEMBER

Soft skills demonstrate that you understand the different characteristics that will help you succeed within an organization and in your specific position. This step is especially important when you don't have a ton of prior work experience. If you look good on paper and sound good in person, your chances of getting hired are greater.

REMEMBER

Be your authentic self both in what you put on your resume and what you demonstrate in the interview!

Looking good on paper: The resume

Because more and more employers today are hiring for attitude, including your soft skills on your resume is more important than ever. Just the fact that you know what soft skills are goes a long way toward impressing potential employers, but tailoring the soft skills on your resume to match the position you're applying for is over-the-top impressive. Customizing your resume to fit the company and job requirements lets potential employers get a look at your specific capabilities and whether they make you the right fit. Check out the latest edition of *Resumes For Dummies* by Laura DeCarlo (Wiley) for a lot more information on this important document.

No one universal resume format is perfect for everyone, which is why I'm not using pages to discuss resume formatting. Literally thousands of resume formats are available online, and they cover the spectrum of job applicant situations: no work experience, some work experience, tons of work experience. Choose one that best highlights your qualifications and make it work for you.

Check out the following online resources for some guidance with preparing your resume:

>> **Resume Now:** https://resume-now.com

>> **My Resume Pros:** https://myresumepros.com

>> **Resume Genius:** https://resumegenius.com

TIP

Look for a format that's easy to edit so you can customize your resume for each job application. As you're preparing your resume, keep the following things in mind:

>> **Showing beats telling:** Everyone can say they have soft skills such as being hardworking, organized, and a team player. The key to a successful resume is to demonstrate or show prospective employers that you have these skills and that you know how to put them to work on the job and in life. Choose one or two soft skills that you think you'd use on the job you're applying for and then give a brief situational example of how you've successfully applied each of these skills in the past.

As a summer camp counselor, I coordinated with 12 other counselors I had just met to provide a safe and engaging experience for all campers.

>> **Taking action:** The words you use when writing your resume are important. Action verbs are more attractive and powerful than the passive version, so when you describe your personal and professional highlights, be sure to use active and successful action words.

I implemented a new cost-cutting procedure for fulfilling customer orders that is still saving the company thousands of dollars a year.

>> **Proofing your fine points:** One of the most common resume mistakes is failing to proofread. When one of your highlighted soft skills is excellent attention to detail, you need to make sure that your resume is pristine. That means checking and then checking again to be sure that you have no spelling

errors, that your contact information is correct, and that you haven't promised anything you can't convincingly sell when your well-researched and well-written resume lands you that all-important personal interview.

Ambition is the path to success. Persistence is the vehicle you arrive in.

—BILL BRADLEY

Looking good in person: The interview

In today's competitive job market, your resume is just the tool that gets you in the door (see the preceding section). The personal interview is what seals the deal. According to business owners and managers, a successful interview is a crucial component of the hiring process. The following sections cover the critical steps you should take before, during, and after a job interview.

Building confidence before the interview

Like with most successful things in life, practice makes perfect. Practicing how to answer typical interview questions helps you learn more about who you are and what type of employee and team player you are. The more you practice your answers, the higher your confidence level rises until you're ready to walk into that interview with your head held high.

Interviewers often ask questions designed to assess your soft skills, and preparing for these questions can help you ace the interview. For example, hiring managers ask behavioral questions to predict how you may react to various situations you encounter on the job. These open-ended questions require more than a yes-or-no answer, which is why they require some preparation. The following are some example prompts/questions to help you get started on your interview preparedness.

1. Tell me about a time you were faced with a difficult work or life situation and what steps you took to solve the problem.

2. Describe an instance where you went above and beyond what a work or life situation required and why you chose to go the extra mile.

3. How do you normally prioritize your work or life tasks?

4. Tell me about a time you disagreed with a decision that was made at work.

5. Describe a time when you made a mistake at work or in life. How did you handle it? What were the results?

Never bend your head. Always hold it high. Look the world straight in the eye.

—HELEN KELLER

Arriving early

Plan to get to your interview ahead of time. After you have a job, showing up on time and ready to work is crucial, and demonstrating that ability from the interview stage is a good start.

Punctuality is a major concern for employers, and rolling into an interview late often kills your chances of landing the job. Getting there 15 minutes early, on the other hand, makes you look as good to a potential employer in person as you did on paper. Maybe even better.

A few days before your interview, make a trial trip to the interviewing location so you know exactly where you're going and how long it takes to get there. You can even scout out a coffee shop or another place to hang out if you arrive more than 15 minutes early.

TIP

You may also want to map an alternate route or two in case you run into a detour or delay the day of. The officers working an accident on the interstate won't know that you have a job interview, so the more you plan ahead the better.

Also make sure you have reliable transportation. If you're getting a ride to your interview, don't ask the friend who arrives late to school every day to be your chauffeur.

Being prepared

Being prepared for a job interview starts with doing your homework. Before you interview with a company, you want to research a little bit about the organization, such as the following information:

>> Key people within the company and owners

>> Size of the company and various departments

>> Products and services provided

>> Customer base (who shops/eats/does business there)

>> Social media presence

Some employers ask you what you know about their business during an interview to gauge your true interest in the job. The more information you've prepared in advance, the better the impression you make on the interviewer. When you do your company research, find out what you can about the position and the company. This step lets you know which personal and professional skills to highlight during your interview.

REMEMBER

All the research in the world doesn't matter, though, if you don't show up on the day with basic supplies. Make sure you bring the following with you to the interview:

>> Completed job application

>> Personal references

>> Resume

>> Working permit, if needed

>> Pen and paper

Your interviewer may not ask to see any of these items, but letting the person know you've brought them with you shows that you understand the concept of being prepared.

Being presentable

Job interviews are like anything else: First impressions have a huge impact. As I explain in Chapter 6, people form a first impression in just four seconds, which means you have very little time to score those all-important first impression points with your interviewer.

Prospective employers are especially attentive to appearance if you're applying for a position in a customer contact position, such as a server, store clerk, receptionist, or front desk worker. The goal is to look the part — to look like the kind of person who the company would be proud to employ and who values themselves and their future career.

TIP

The interview isn't the time to make a bold fashion statement. Choose your interview attire ahead of time, and make sure that it's clean and pressed the night before.

Minding your manners

Along with your physical appearance (which I cover in the preceding section), manners and body language send a strong first message. And not just to your interviewer.

REMEMBER

The interview process starts the second you step foot on the company's property. The receptionist, secretary, or staff member who greets you may not be your interviewer, but you can bet that after you've come and gone, the interviewer will inquire about the kind of first impression you made on your potential co-workers.

The more energy, enthusiasm, and positive attitude you display, the better your first impression. Employers want upbeat workers who don't bring personal drama and negativity to the workplace. While waiting to be called into your interview, sit up straight and lean slightly forward to show you're ready and eager to impress.

Being a closer

In most cases, after your interviewer has asked the last question, they'll turn the interview over to you. This opportunity is your moment to show that you're well prepared to prove that you'll be an asset to the company. At this point in the interview, your soft skills get to take the stage:

>> Ask a few informed questions about the job, such as about the nature of the work, training programs, supervision, clientele, and when they expect to make a decision on filling the position.

>> Don't ask how much the position pays. If and when you're offered the job, that's the time to talk money. Sure, you want to get paid, but you don't want to leave your interviewer with the final impression that you're only interested in what you can get rather than what you can give.

>> If it seems like a good fit, look the interviewer confidently in the eye and tell them you really want to work there.

TIP

On the other hand, if you reach the end of the interview and have already determined the position wouldn't be a good fit for you, consider letting the interviewer know right away. Politely telling the interviewer that you're not the right candidate for the job enables them to focus their attention and hiring efforts on other applicants.

>> Close your interview strong with a handshake and a smile. Thank the interviewer for their time, the opportunity to learn more about the company, and the invitation to meet in person.

Following up on the interview

What you do after your personal interview can separate you from the rest of the job candidates. Start with a formal and timely follow-up thank-you email expressing your gratitude for the interview, stating briefly that you'd love to work for the company, and indicating why you think you're a good fit. This gesture reminds your interviewer that you understand punctuality, responsibility, and good manners and that you know how to get things done.

You can also follow up with a phone call. When leaving a voicemail, keep it brief and polite. A few sentences, ending with something positive such as "I look forward to hearing from you in the near future" can suffice.

THE PARABLE OF THE PENCIL

The Pencil Maker took the pencil aside just before putting it into the box. "You need to know five things," said the Pencil Maker, "before I send you out into the world. Always remember them, and you'll become the best pencil you can be.

1. You'll be able to do many great things, but only if you allow yourself to be held in someone's hand.

2. You'll experience a painful sharpening from time to time, but you'll need it to become a better pencil.

3. You'll be able to correct any mistakes you may make.

4. The most important part of you will always be what's inside.

5. On every surface you're used on, you must leave your mark. No matter what the condition, you must continue to write."

The pencil understood and promised to remember, and it went into the box with purpose in its heart.

4

The Part of Tens

Chapter **14**

Ten Inspiring Soft Skills Phrases

Sometimes a little inspiration helps when the going gets tough in the workplace and in life. In this chapter, I offer a list of ten popular, practical, and easy-to-remember soft skills phrases that can help you stay positive and motivated on your journey to career and life success. You can even use them to offer inspiration to others along the way.

These ten simple but very powerful and positive phrases can serve as daily reminders to help you create the job, life, and relationships you want. Write them down, pin them up, and give them a second look whenever you need a lift. I'm sharing them to help you get from where you are to where you want to be!

Soft Skills Make the Hard Skills Work

As I explain in Chapter 1, *hard skills* are what you do, and *soft skills* are how you do what you do. When you combine technical ability with strong interpersonal skills such as attitude, character, communication, time management, and a solid work ethic, your potential for career and life success grows by leaps and bounds.

Soft skills can be more difficult to acquire than hard skills because they're more subjective and have more shades of gray than hard skills. But you need to develop them because today's employers hire for soft skills and train for hard skills because they know the value soft skills have in making the workplace operate successfully.

Soft skills do more than improve your performance and opportunity for success in the workplace. They also improve your personal performance and opportunity for success and happiness in your life outside work.

Your Attitude Determines Your Altitude

You make a choice each day about what kind of attitude you're going to present to the world. Your attitude sets your direction, impacts the choices you make, and affects how people respond to you. Sometimes you need to check and adjust your attitude throughout the day if you sense it's getting off track.

REMEMBER

A positive attitude attracts. With a positive attitude, you attract good things, such as jobs, friends, and the respect of others. A positive attitude can turn a gray day sunny. (Metaphorically, that is. It won't actually blow the clouds out of the sky.) It can turn a frown upside down. It can draw opportunity and possibility to you like a magnet.

Conversely, a negative attitude can repel good things because you can't see them as they come your way. The glass is always half empty. The sky stays gray, and the frown stays down. If negative things are all you perceive, that's often what you get in return: negativity.

You're the boss of your attitude, so whether you put effort into trying to maintain a positive attitude is up to you. Just know that working hard to have a positive attitude can affect how high you can climb. Your attitude determines your altitude.

Look the Part; Act the Part; Get the Part

You may have heard people say, "Dress for the job you want, not the job you have." That's another way of saying that when you look the part, others tend to give you and your ideas more respect and take you more seriously. When you act the part, you're showing and selling your value. You're demonstrating that you're qualified, ready to lead, and confident. When you have looking the part and acting the part in place, you're more likely to get the part!

Listen as Well as You Hear

There's a big difference between hearing and listening, as I note in Chapter 4. Your ears give you the ability to hear, but good communication is more than just picking up on the sounds around you. Listening is what happens when you truly connect and communicate with others with your entire person.

REMEMBER

Life has always been busy, but today people have more things competing for their attention than ever before. Communication is evolving and changing quickly, and with mobile devices sending notifications of texts, tweets, and snaps, you may often use your eyes more than your ears to communicate with others. However, you can't let listening take a back seat on today's superfast information and communication highway. Active listening needs to ride shotgun.

Listening is the path to understanding so communication can be actionable and insightful. You can't practice how your ears process sound, but you can and should hone your active listening skills so you can receive the messages others are delivering to you.

Thinking Is Critical

Critical thinking is the ability to absorb important information and use it to form your own opinions and make your own decisions in life and at work. (You can read more about critical thinking in Chapter 9.) Many of the greatest achievers in the world are great because they've learned to ask effective questions that have encouraged critical thinking.

Employers highly regard people who can think critically to solve problems. When you can think independently, separate fact from opinion, and ask questions, you're showing critical thinking skills that contribute to workplace success.

Manage Your Time, or It Will Manage You

Good time management isn't about how much you have to do in a day. It's about what you accomplish.

Strong time management skills allow you to be focused and fully present in whatever activity you're currently engaging in. When your time is managing you, you're always running late, and you probably find that you're unable to give your current task your full focus because you're already worried about the next item on your list. You may end up with one thing that never gets done because you never have enough time in the day to get to it.

When you take control of your schedule and figure out how to be disciplined with your time management, you discover how much you've been missing at work and in life. Managing your time frees up time for you to be creative and proactive with your work and life goals. You're able to achieve much more than when you allow your schedule to run you ragged, and you'll finally be able to get to that one thing. Chapter 7 has more info on time management.

Hard Work Makes Life Easier

The people who most often achieve and enjoy the best things in life are those who have a "no matter what it takes" work ethic. They give their all every day in every way. They put everything they have into achieving their goals, whether that's starting a business, getting to the finish line of a 10K, or graduating first in their class. High performers are dedicated to hard work and excellence, and as a result, the quality of their personal and professional lives usually is also excellent.

The harder you work to cultivate a good work ethic, the easier and more enjoyable life can be. The internal and external rewards that come from working hard professionally often lead to career and personal happiness and success. I cover work ethic in more detail in Chapter 10.

Character Counts

Good character is made up of positive personality traits such as honesty, courage, integrity, and loyalty. When a person has good character, it shows in their actions. You can see it in the daily choices they make, the way they treat other people, and the actions they take. For an in-depth discussion of character, head to Chapter 3.

TIP

Stay focused on how you put your character on public display every day and on what that character is telling other people about you. If you say you're going to be somewhere at a certain time, be there at that time. If you agree to join an organization and volunteer, show up and contribute. If you say you'll do something, do it to the best of your ability.

A Lot of Different Flowers Make a Bouquet

How you choose to respond to the cultural differences you encounter every day has a huge impact on your future success. In Chapter 5, I discuss how tempting the seeming comfort of hanging out and working with people who are just like you can be. But keeping yourself insulated from people who are different from you diminishes the potential for work and life effectiveness and enjoyment — plus, you miss out on so much!

Inside or outside the workplace, teams are more interesting and successful when they're groups of diverse people with unique perspectives, experiences, cultural backgrounds, and expertise. Celebrate diversity and differences, and everyone is more likely to be happier.

Teamwork Makes the Dream Work

It takes a team to achieve a dream. The most successful outcomes happen when people come together to contribute their ideas to create and develop projects that accomplish the team goals. It's called synergy! You can't have synergy without team members who show up, speak up, and step up. Read more about teamwork in Chapter 8.

IN THIS CHAPTER

» Improving soft skills through practice
and research

» Taking your soft skills into new
territory

» Assessing goals and rewarding
achievements

Chapter 15

Ten Ways to Grow Your Soft Skills

As you get more and more in touch with the person and employee you want to be, you find that work and life offer you daily situations and opportunities to develop your soft skills both personally and professionally. In this chapter, I offer ten strategies to help keep you moving forward on the path to career and life success.

Practice Makes Perfect

Practice makes perfect. Each week, pick one soft skill and dedicate yourself to practicing that skill each day. Pretty soon, you'll notice a marked improvement in that skill, and so will those around you.

Do Some Research

Curiosity is a soft skill, and the more you learn, the more you grow. This book is just the tip of the iceberg for cultivating a strong set of soft skills. You can find all kinds of sources that can help you hone your soft skills set: the Internet, the library, bookstores. Look for resources on soft skills in general and how to apply them in specific instances, or dig a little deeper into individual skills, such as communication and critical thinking.

REMEMBER

Additional research and training are especially important for any soft skills you feel are weaknesses. If you're not sure where you need the most help, check out the self-assessments in Chapters 2 through 11. Those checkups of each skill can help you determine which of your soft skills need the most attention.

Ask for Feedback

Sometimes knowing whether you're growing or where you need to improve is difficult. If you're not sure where you stand on the soft skills scale, getting feedback can help. You can ask a trusted friend or co-worker for their opinion on your grasp of certain skills. You can also ask your employer for a review and for suggestions on how you can continue to improve your soft skills set. You don't have to go it alone!

WARNING

Don't ask for feedback just to get compliments (although you should definitely accept them if you receive them). You're looking for honest guidance to help you continue to grow, so getting defensive or angry if someone points out an area where you can improve isn't appropriate.

Sign Up for Classes

All kinds of online programs and classes focus on self-improvement in general and soft skills and professional development in particular. Your local community college is a great place to find adult learning opportunities such as weekend workshops and lectures, and many are free to the public. Try searching **soft skills training** to find results for both online and in-person classes.

Set New Goals

The best way to keep growing is to keep setting new goals for yourself. Make sure you set achievable targets, though. If you have a big goal, break it down into a series of smaller ones that keep moving you toward the finish line. Otherwise, you may set off at a sprint and become discouraged before you can realize the ultimate goal.

For example, maybe you want to get to work early each day to get a head start. Begin with 30 minutes each morning for the first week. At the end of the week, take a look back and chart your progress and your results.

TIP

Try making a list of five things you want to achieve at work or in your personal life and set appropriate goals. You can't go anywhere standing still!

Join the Party

Most companies have regular activities and events scheduled for their employees. Some are just for fun, and some are offered as training and promotion opportunities. The best way to continue to grow as an employee and a person is to be a joiner! You can not only meet new people and learn new things but also practice all your soft skills in the process. And you just may have some fun!

Instead of racing out to your car at the end of the day, take a minute to check out the breakroom bulletin board for upcoming activities and events. You can also check out your community bulletin board for events, activities, sports leagues, and volunteer opportunities, which are all good places to practice your soft skills

Take Inventory

Every once in a while, stop on your career and life journey and take a little personal and professional inventory. How's your time management? Does your attitude need an adjustment? Does your work ethic need a little push? *Remember:* Taking inventory can show you where you need to improve, but it can also show you where you're shining! Taking the good with the not-quite-there-yet makes continuing on your career and life success journey with new inspiration easier.

TIP

Write down the ten crucial soft skills (see Chapter 1) and rate yourself for each on a scale of 1 (need lots of help) to 10 (crushing it). You can also find online assessments. Try doing an Internet search for **soft skills assessment questionnaire** to find an interactive set of questions.

Get Comfortable Being Uncomfortable

To a certain extent, having a comfort zone is fine. When it comes to growing, however, things are supposed to get a little uncomfortable. One way to hone your soft skills is to step out of your comfort zone and interact with people and situations that challenge you personally and professionally. Getting comfortable with being uncomfortable sharpens your soft skills set and widens your world. The good news is that stepping out of your comfort zone is only uncomfortable at the start. After you're out there, you discover it feels just fine!

Try, Try Again

Ever tried. Ever failed. No matter. Try again. Fail again. Fail better.

—SAMUEL BECKETT

Failure is a part of life. When you get something wrong, see it as an opportunity to get it right the next time you try it. Late for work this morning? Stay late this afternoon. Didn't play well with others today? Say you're sorry and be nicer tomorrow.

REMEMBER

Failure is a learning experience, not a life sentence. Don't beat yourself up when you fall down. It happens. Just get back up, mentally brush yourself off, apply your critical thinking and problem-solving soft skills to the situation, and start all over again.

Reward Yourself

When your soft skills are working, give yourself a pat on the back and a little reward for a job well done. Celebrating when you get it right is important, and you don't need to wait for someone else to recognize how well you're doing. You need to appreciate yourself, too. It helps keep you motivated to continue to get it right so that you just want to keep right on going and growing.

Index

A

A+ attitude. *See* positive attitude
accountability
  in time management, 92
  in work ethic, 129–130
acquiring soft skills, 8, 14
acting the part, 82–84, 168. *See also* etiquette
action words, in resume, 159
active listening. *See* listening
activities, participating in company
  bettering attitude by, 24
  growing soft skills by, 175
adjusting attitude, 22–25
adversity affirmations, 28
advising, as disconnection block, 53
affirmations, positive, 27–29
AHA (American Hospitality Academy), 74–75
altitude, attitude as determining, 20, 168
Altshuler, Michael, 93
America Succeeds, 121–122
American Hospitality Academy (AHA), 74–75
Angelou, Maya, 42
anger, 42
apathy, 42
appearance
  four-second first impressions, 78–79
  importance of, 81–82
  incorporating into daily life, 151
  for interviews, 162
  and leadership, 136
  overview, 10, 77
  real-life scenarios, 84–85
  self-assessment, 79–80
aptitude, versus attitude, 9, 155
arriving early for interview, 161
arrogance, 42

artistic career personality types, 156
asking
  for feedback, 174
  questions, as critical thinking skill, 115–117
assessing soft skills
  appearance and etiquette, 79–80
  attitude, 21–22
  character, 37–38
  communication, 50–51
  critical thinking, 113
  leadership, 134–135
  overview, 175
  stereotyping, 71–72
  teamwork, 101–103
  time management, 88–90
  using to improve soft skills, 174
  work ethic, 124–125
assumptions, evaluating, 117. *See also* critical
   thinking
attitude
  adjusting, 22–25
  versus aptitude, 9, 155
  versus character, 35
  choosing, 22–23, 29
  as determining altitude, 20, 168
  developing positive
   being your own best friend, 29
   challenging yourself, 26
   overview, 25
   with positive affirmations, 27–29
   simple ways to nurture, 25–26
  exercise to build good, 30–33
  finding positive spin on situations, 30
  importance of, 18–20
  incorporating into daily life, 150
  and leadership, 136
  offsetting negativity of others, 24–25

real-life scenarios *(continued)*

  critical thinking, 120–121

  cultural awareness, 73–74

  leadership, 140–141

  teamwork, 108

  time management, 96

  work ethic, 131

reason, being moved by, 118

rectangle personality shape, 105

refocusing attention, in verbal communication, 58–59

rehearsing, as disconnection block, 53

relationships, soft skills indicating maintenance of, 157–158

reliability, as trait related to good work ethic, 126

Remember icon, explained, 2

remote working, soft skills important for, 34

repeating main idea, in verbal communication, 58

reputation, versus character, 40

research

  for interview, 161–162

  role in growing soft skills, 173–174

respect. *See also* cultural awareness

  as character trait, 41

  in cultural awareness, 73

  in verbal communication, 58

responsibility

  as character trait, 41

  as trait related to good work ethic, 127

resume, including soft skills on, 158–160

reversing negative thinking with positive affirmations, 27–29

rewarding yourself for growing soft skills, 176

RIASEC model, 156–157

Roosevelt, Eleanor, 130, 154

routines, daily, 91. *See also* time management

rudeness, 42

S

scales, soft skill. *See* self-assessment

scheduling, 91. *See also* time management

self-assessment

  appearance and etiquette, 79–80

  attitude, 21–22

  character, 37–38

  communication, 50–51

  critical thinking, 113

  leadership, 134–135

  of soft skills, 175

  stereotyping, 71–72

  teamwork, 101–103

  time management, 88–90

  using to improve soft skills, 174

  work ethic, 124–125

self-awareness

  as core critical thinking skill, 118

  and work ethic, 130

self-discipline

  in time management, 92

  as trait related to good work ethic, 126

self-esteem affirmations, 28

self-motivation, 127

self-talk, positive, 27–29

separating fact from opinion, 115

shaking hands, 83

shapes, personality, 104–106, 108

Shaw, George Bernard, 80

Short, Stephanie, 121–122

SHRM (Society for Human Resource Management), 34

simplicity, in verbal communication, 58

small goals, role in positive attitude, 26

small wins, role in positive attitude, 26

smiling

  role in appearance, 81

  role in positive attitude, 26

Smith, Stan, 132

smoothing over, as disconnection block, 53

social career personality types, 156

Society for Human Resource Management (SHRM), 34

Socrates, 112

soft skills

  applying to work and life, 13–14

  defined, 8–9

  essential, 9–11

  growing, 173–176

  importance of, 11–13

  incorporating into daily life, 149–154

  inspiring phrases related to, 167–171

  learning, 8, 14

  overview, 1–3, 7, 145

  personal responsibility for, 14–15

  self-assessment, 175

  showing off to prospective employers, 155

    interview, 160–164

    overview, 157–158

    resume, 158–160

  taking personally, 145–149

solving problems effectively, 118–120. *See also* critical thinking

sparring, as disconnection block, 53

speaking. *See also* communication

  energy put into way of, 81

  from heart, 55

speed, in vocal communication, 57

spin, positive, 30

square personality shape, 105

squiggle personality shape, 106

Stan Smith Events, 132

Stanley Black & Decker, 60

staying on point, in verbal communication, 58

stepping out of comfort zone

  cultural, 65

  importance, 176

stereotyping. *See also* bias; cultural awareness

  overview, 70–71

  real-life scenarios, 74

  recognizing, 72–73

  self-assessment, 71–72

strategic problem-solving, 118–120. *See also* critical thinking

students, learning of soft skills by, 8

subjective soft skills, 8–9

suspected aspects of culture, 66–67. *See also* cultural awareness

synergy, 171. *See also* teamwork

T

talk, walking your, 59, 84

talking, after listening, 52. *See also* communication

teamwork

  building strong team, 103–104

  cooperation and conflict management, 106–107

  and ego, 100

  importance of, 100, 171

  incorporating into daily life, 152

  and leadership, 136–137

  measurement of by prospective employers, 157

  overview, 10, 99

  and personality shapes, 104–106

  real-life scenarios, 108

  self-assessment, 101–103

thinking independently, 114–115. *See also* critical thinking

The Three Bricklayers story, 23

three Vs of communication

  improving, 55–59

  overview, 54–55

time for yourself, taking, 25

time management

  importance of, 169–170

  incorporating into daily life, 151–152

  and leadership, 136

  overview, 10, 87

  real-life scenarios, 96

  self-assessment, 88–90

  spending time wisely, 88

  taking control of

    becoming manager of your minutes, 93–96

    excuses, giving up, 93

    overview, 90

    trading being busy for being productive, 90–93

Tip icon, explained, 2

to-do lists, 94

training, role in growing soft skills, 174

About the Author

Cindi Reiman is the president and founder of the American Hospitality Academy and Soft Skills AHA. Since 1986, the American Hospitality Academy, in partnership with premier resorts and hotels throughout the United States, has been the bridge between colleges and industry, providing career-focused soft skills curriculum and structured training for thousands of students and young adults. Through this close working relationship with top industry leaders, Cindi and her team developed an appreciation for and clear understanding of how to best teach the 21st century soft skills that are essential to career and life success.

In 2005, in partnership with the American Hotel and Lodging Association, AHA created the college internship manual SERVLEAD (Service Leadership in a Multicultural Workplace). This comprehensive and first-of-its-kind soft skills manual provided professional development and leadership coursework, training competencies, and an industry certification to students who successfully completed the program.

In 2018, Cindi launched Soft Skills AHA, a series of online development programs designed to meet the demand of companies around the world that more and more are hiring for attitude and training for aptitude. Soft Skills AHA's engaging career readiness curriculum and positive online learning environment emphasizes the essential employability traits necessary to be successful both in the workplace and in life.

Forever dedicated to bridging the gap between what is taught in the classroom and what industry requires in the workplace, Soft Skills AHA online programs now provide education to students in both middle school and high school, teaching the essential skills that employers look for when hiring new graduates. Soft Skills AHA also works with workforce development organizations to prepare young people to enter the workforce.

To learn more, visit www.softkskillsaha.com.

Author's Acknowledgments

When Jennifer from the *For Dummies* team called, I was so excited for the opportunity to write this book. The truth is it has actually been 36 years in the making. Not the writing, but the research. As founder and president of the American Hospitality Academy, I have spent more than 30 fun and exciting years developing our signature Amazing Hospitality Attitude (aha) in-person and online programs for college interns, workforce, and high school and middle school students.

I realized early in my career that companies expect employees to know what soft skills are and how to demonstrate them in the workplace. Sadly, students rarely do, because these essential career and life skills are not typically taught in school. It is my hope that this book helps bridge the gap between what readers learned in school and what they need to know on the job. I hope during the process, each reader develops their own aha and has a little fun on the journey to career and life success.

I would like to thank first and foremost Katie Huffstetler, who started out as an intern with the American Hospitality Academy more than 27 years ago and has become one of my closest friends and my absolute best teammate. This book and all the training programs we have developed over the years would not have been possible without Katie's passion, creativity, and dedication to the development of our students.

To Cora Gatchalian, thank you for your wealth of academic knowledge and incredible support, friendship, and belief in me and AHA over the years.

To Karin Morrison and the AHA team, thanks for your unwavering dedication to cultural exchange, making a difference in the lives of our students, and being such incredible role models for them and an inspiration for me.

To April Burns and Karen Ann Wapole, thanks for being there in the beginning of RRTM as our original CEOs — Chief Energizing Officers — and getting our management team and our interns *revved up, ready to go, and totally motivated!*

To Cindy Whitman, thank you for your amazing writing skills and for being such an incredible copy editor for me and AHA over the years. Your inspirational and fun writing style has provided the perfect "voice" for our training courses and this book.

To my family and friends, thanks for always putting up with my constant efforts to try to explain the term *soft skills.* This book's for you!

And finally, to Greg Goldberg, my best friend and biggest fan. There is no one who genuinely displays and practices soft skills day in and day out the way you do. Thanks for always being there and for supporting me in all the many endeavors I have embarked on over the years. You have made all of them so much more fun.

Publisher's Acknowledgments

Acquisitions Editor: Jennifer Yee

Project Editor: Charlotte Kughen

Copy Editor: Megan Knoll

Technical Editor: Rebecca Bollwitt

Sr. Editorial Assistant: Cherie Case

Production Editor: Mohammed Zafar Ali

Cover Image: © Zivica Kerkez/Shutterstock

Take dummies with you everywhere you go!

Whether you are excited about e-books, want more from the web, must have your mobile apps, or are swept up in social media, dummies makes everything easier.

Find us online!

dummies.com

dummies

A Wiley Brand

Leverage the power

Dummies is the global leader in the reference category and one of the most trusted and highly regarded brands in the world. No longer just focused on books, customers now have access to the dummies content they need in the format they want. Together we'll craft a solution that engages your customers, stands out from the competition, and helps you meet your goals.

Advertising & Sponsorships

Connect with an engaged audience on a powerful multimedia site, and position your message alongside expert how-to content. Dummies.com is a one-stop shop for free, online information and know-how curated by a team of experts.

- Targeted ads
- Video
- Email Marketing
- Microsites
- Sweepstakes sponsorship

20 MILLION
PAGE VIEWS
EVERY SINGLE MONTH

15 MILLION
UNIQUE
VISITORS PER MONTH

43%
OF ALL VISITORS
ACCESS THE SITE
VIA THEIR MOBILE DEVICES

700,000 NEWSLETTER SUBSCRIPTIONS
TO THE INBOXES OF
300,000 UNIQUE INDIVIDUALS EVERY WEEK

# of dummies

Custom Publishing

Reach a global audience in any language by creating a solution that will differentiate you from competitors, amplify your message, and encourage customers to make a buying decision.

- Apps
- Books
- eBooks
- Video
- Audio
- Webinars

Brand Licensing & Content

Leverage the strength of the world's most popular reference brand to reach new audiences and channels of distribution.

For more information, visit dummies.com/biz

Learning Made Easy

ACADEMIC

9781119293576
USA $19.99
CAN $23.99
UK £15.99

9781119293637
USA $19.99
CAN $23.99
UK £15.99

9781119293491
USA $19.99
CAN $23.99
UK £15.99

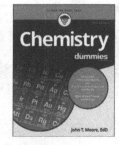
9781119293460
USA $19.99
CAN $23.99
UK £15.99

9781119293590
USA $19.99
CAN $23.99
UK £15.99

9781119215844
USA $26.99
CAN $31.99
UK £19.99

9781119293378
USA $22.99
CAN $27.99
UK £16.99

9781119293521
USA $19.99
CAN $23.99
UK £15.99

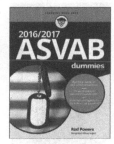
9781119239178
USA $18.99
CAN $22.99
UK £14.99

9781119263883
USA $26.99
CAN $31.99
UK £19.99

Available Everywhere Books Are Sold

Small books for big imaginations

9781119177173
USA $9.99
CAN $9.99
UK £8.99

9781119177272
USA $9.99
CAN $9.99
UK £8.99

9781119177241
USA $9.99
CAN $9.99
UK £8.99

9781119177210
USA $9.99
CAN $9.99
UK £8.99

9781119262657
USA $9.99
CAN $9.99
UK £6.99

9781119291336
USA $9.99
CAN $9.99
UK £6.99

9781119233527
USA $9.99
CAN $9.99
UK £6.99

9781119291220
USA $9.99
CAN $9.99
UK £6.99

9781119177302
USA $9.99
CAN $9.99
UK £8.99

Unleash Their Creativity